D1084164

Epstein Once upon an Alp

Cover design and illustrations by Hans Kuechler

Eugene V. Epstein

Once upon an Alp

Further Tales of Life in Switzerland
By the Author of

Lend Me Your Alphorn

Benteli

Layout and printing by Benteli Inc., Berne
Printed in Switzerland

ISBN 3-7165-0252-9

Contents

“*En Suisse, on trouve beaucoup de montagnes.*”

—Voltaire

Preface

Watches the Swiss export to all parts of the world; humorists they have to import. I feel profound admiration for Eugene V. Epstein that he was brave enough to consent – indeed: he was eager – to be imported to Switzerland as a humorous writer.
Few people understand the reasons, but I do because I happen to know his birthplace, Long Island, U.S.A. He alleges – and as he is the soul of veracity I must believe him – that Long Island was a peaceful and charming place when he was born there. Well, everything is possible. Today it is part of Suburbia, a mess of ugly houses, a sea of pomposity, self-satisfaction and neurosis. So he packed his suitcase and fled. Originally a music critic, he found himself in Switzerland, the land of yodelling and of the *Alphorn*. Such an experience is likely to turn anyone into a humorist; if, on top of it all, somebody spends two years working for the American Military Intelligence, the result is inevitable. Mr. Epstein started laughing at the world and has not stopped ever since.
I have deep sympathy for Mr. Epstein, as I have had my own encounters with the Swiss sense of humour at its most terrifying. A few years ago I was asked by a Swiss organisation to make a satirical, leg-pulling film on Switzerland. I warned

the gentleman in question that a satirical film might, in fact, be satirical and the Swiss might not like it. He started shouting at me, stating furiously that the Swiss have an exquisite sense of humour, that they are, indeed, extremely light-hearted and hilarious, and I should go ahead. I went ahead, and when the film – altogether a rather mild and harmless affair – was ready, the head of that organisation hid it in the vaults and safes and no one ever saw it again.

It may well be the case, simply, that the Swiss – an intelligent and perceptive nation – prefer Mr. Epstein's humour to mine. I do not blame them for this. He makes fun of the Swiss love for yodelling and sausages which goes down well with the Swiss; making fun of sausages, quite frankly, does not go down equally well with me because I love and respect sausages – I revere sausages – and I want everybody to take them seriously. I have absolutely no sense of humour as far as sausages are concerned. Mr. Epstein, on other occasions, skates on thinner ice. He mocks the Swiss love for their card-game, *Jass*, and speaks disrespectfully of *Kirsch*. I think this is dangerous and I doubt if the Swiss are going to take it.

I especially liked his theory about the *Föhn* – the warm south wind – about which I heard so much but which I never really experienced. People were knocked out left and right and told me with deep sighs that there was a *Föhn* on. I never noticed anything; neither did Mr. Epstein. To his great glory, he discovered the truth. There is no such thing as *Föhn*. It is simply a universal excuse for laziness and mistakes. Other lands have other excuses, the Swiss have the *Föhn*. Or rather they do not have the *Föhn*, that's Mr. Epstein's whole point.

By now Mr. Epstein must have discovered that in one respect he made a mistake when he exchanged the United States for Switzerland. Racial tension is much worse in Switzerland. It is true that its manifestations are milder, more civilised, much less violent. But the tension itself is worse. The fact that all Swiss are of the same colour should not mislead anyone. If I may commit the unforgivable sin of quoting myself: "The human soul needs to get rid of a certain amount of hatred and nastiness just as an internal combustion engine must get rid of a certain amount of poisonous gas. The Swiss get rid of these gases by despising each other so intensely that they have no energy to spare for the rest of humanity." But perhaps as long as the people of Basle do not march on Zurich, causing race riots there, we needn't worry unduly.

Perhaps this is true. Perhaps this is the reason why the Swiss succeeded in building a country and a society which Mr. Epstein (and, I confess,

I too) love so much. On the other hand it is quite possible that one or two of my references are unfair or downright unjust to the Swiss. Well, there is a *Föhn* on.

George Mikes

Once upon an Alp

Once upon a time, high upon a Swiss alp, there lived a family of Swiss farmers named Obenamberg. Father Obenamberg, called "Seppli" by the villagers, was a hard-working, clean-living man of sixty-two, who got up every morning at half past three to attend to the many chores of his farm, which was perched lazily on the steep slopes of the alp.

It was a rich alp, abundant with flowers in the spring, with fine, nourishing grass for the cows. Farmer Obenamberg's cows were healthy and gave pure, creamy milk, like milk should be in Switzerland. Seppli's family consisted of two children, Heidi and Gottfried, and a wife, one of the most prominent suffragettes of Eastern Switzerland. Heidi was a charming child when she was very young – just like the fabled Heidi of the book. Gottfried, at the age of seven, looked like William Tell, except for the beard, which Gottfried didn't grow until he was nearly twelve.

Gottfried loved the farm life above the village of Strampelhosen, where his family had lived for generations. From the very beginning, he loved to help around the house and the farm. He would often lead his father's cows high up on the lush alp, where the grass was always greener and the resulting milk still milkier. As he grew older, Gottfried

learned to perform the more difficult tasks – like collecting manure and placing it on a pile in front of the house. Seppli and Gottfried were proud of their manure pile, the largest and most pungent within twenty-seven kilometers. Seppli knew that some of his countrymen were renowned for the size of their numbered bank accounts, but for Seppli wealth was a manure pile, and Gottfried was the bookkeeper.

It was a placid existence, this alpine life. There were no neuroses, no anxiety, on Gottfried's alp, just flowers and sunshine and some indolent horseflies who buzzed around the big manure pile on brilliant summer days.

One afternoon, not long after his seventeenth birthday, Gottfried made his way down into Strampelhosen to buy some *Kräuterschnaps* for Father Seppli. There, in front of the local Gasthaus, he noticed a great commotion. As he approached, he heard the mayor announce to the villagers that a group of Zurich businessmen had decided to finance a new ski resort in and around the sleepy town. Gottfried's jaw dropped, and he lost the cigar he was smoking. "Ski resort," he murmured to himself. "Finally something's happening around this dull hayseed of a town!"

Gottfried was beside himself. He could hardly believe the news and rushed back up the alp to tell his father, completely forgetting the *Kräuter-*

schnaps. Along the way, he dreamt of the day when Strampelhosen would be as famous as Davos and Zermatt and Herrliberg. He imagined himself as Strampelhosen's foremost ski teacher, wearing a brownish-red jacket with an emblem on it.

Gottfried began to study hard in his free time, for if he wanted to be a ski instructor, with pupils from all over the world, he would have to learn many things. First, he would have to learn to ski and to do the Wiggle and the Waggle and the downhill Columbina, and all the other ornate turns and stops he had seen on Swiss television. And he would have to learn to speak English and French and German.

By the time the new resort had been established, Gottfried had, in fact, become Strampelhosen's authentic expert, thanks largely to the many books on skiing and mountaineering he ordered from a publishing company in London. Now, as the late autumn days grew shorter and the sun dimmed behind the Hornhorn mountain, Gottfried had only to wait for the first good snow.

When the snow came, Gottfried couldn't wait to rip off his tattered overalls and put on the stretch pants and the brownish-red jacket with the emblem on it. A pair of goggles he had ordered from Dortmund and a gay, tasseled hat completed the picture: Gottfried was now Freddy, popular ski

instructor of the Strampelhosen Ski School. His first class that first morning was made up of Americans who had flown over on one of the package tours organized by Trans Liechtenstein Airlines.
Freddy was the hit of the season, both as a glamorous skier and as a dashing socialite after sundown. He soon knew all the princes and sheiks by their first names and was the toast of the *après-ski* set. He was deeply tanned and athletic-looking, and had begun to smoke a pipe. There were constant demands for private lessons with Freddy, especially from American college girls, who thought he was as handsome a ski instructor as Switzerland had ever produced. He even had an offer from a film company, which, good Swiss that he was, he refused when he learned they wanted him to advertise Japanese-made safety bindings. His book, *How to Ski Like Me*, was an international sensation, and had already gone into its sixth printing.

Freddy could dance the twist, the frug and the letkiss until dawn in the rustic village Gasthaus, now known as the "Snow Star Chalet & Grill Room". He was in his element singing "I Been Workin' on the Railroad" and "Trink, trink, Brüderlein, trink" – an international life if ever one existed.

And in the morning, Freddy was always as fresh as edelweiss, as though the evening before were but a dream. One day, as he led his class *schussing* down the alp past his father's farm, he noticed little buds of early crocuses pushing their delicate colors up through the thinning blanket of snow. There was an unmistakable sparkle of spring in the air, and soon rivulets began to appear where only streams of ice had been before.

The first – and eminently successful – winter sports season at Strampelhosen was drawing to a close. Soon the last tourist had packed and sent off his skis and the new hotels were preparing to close up until later in the year.

Gottfried put his tattered overalls back on and walked solemnly into the old barn. His pitchfork was still there, leaning against the wall, where he had left it in November. He grabbed the fork with both hands and dug into an imaginary pile of manure near the stable, and threw what would have been a mighty load in the direction of a hay-wagon which wasn't there. With his right foot he indignantly kicked a battered tin can out through the barn door and into the spring sunshine.

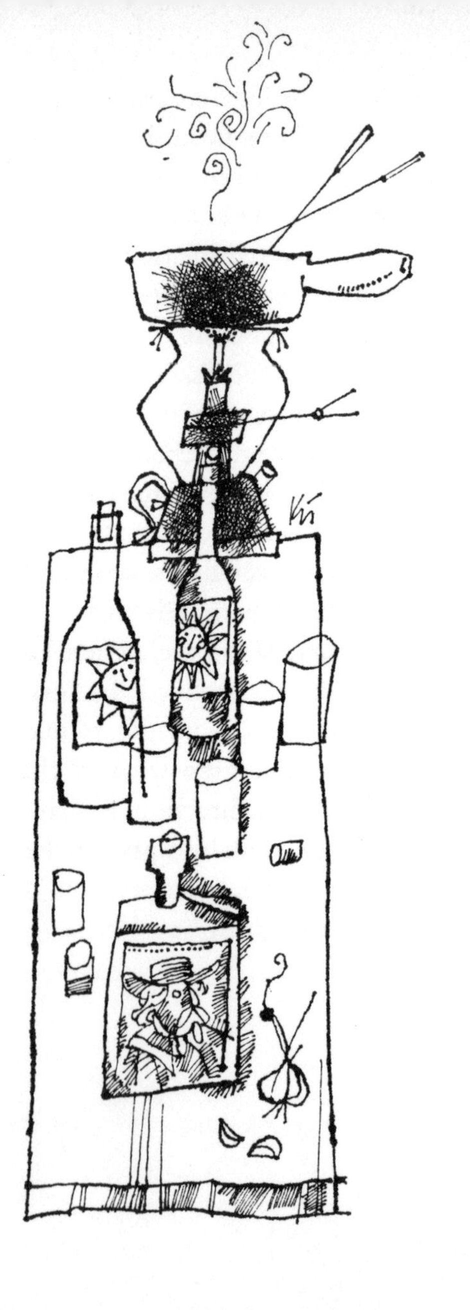

The Fondue File

Of the 2157 restaurants in the immediate vicinity of our home near Zurich, more than half are named *Zum Rössli*, or "At the Sign of the Little Horse". This leads many foreigners to the fallacious conclusion that all these eating places are under the same management. One American friend of ours – who noticed the *Rössli* phenomenon – thought of starting a new chain of restaurants in Switzerland called *Zum Howard Johnson's*, with the intention of making life easier for the increasing number of tourists from the United States.

"Anyway," he said, "Switzerland could use a restaurant serving 28 flavors of ice cream – one flavor for each canton."

I reminded him that, fine as the idea was, there were unfortunately only 25 Swiss cantons. Thus he would either have to reduce the number of flavors or increase the size of Switzerland.

Our friend remained unimpressed, adding that America was far smaller before the Gadsden Purchase and the addition of Alaska and Hawaii as States of the Union. "Foresight," he said, "that's what counts these days, and pity those who don't think ahead. Businesses or countries, they're all the same when you come right down to it!"

Returning to the subject, I assured him that as far

as cuisine was concerned, Switzerland was always thinking ahead. Take the example of *fondue*, which everyone thinks of when the first touch of winter creeps across the land. There was a time – not many Swiss winters ago – when *fondue* meant a melted cheese specialty and nothing else. But this has changed with the advent of prosperity for all. Now there are many kinds of *fondue*, cheese and otherwise, dispensed from chafing dishes bubbling away on the table, all designed to confuse the already confused tourist. It is for this reason that the Swiss Department of Public Information, in conjunction with the Emmentaler Division of the Agriculture Department, has decided to conduct a series of round-table discussions on the future and geopolitical importance of the common *fondue*. We had the good fortune to be invited to the opening talk of the series and are pleased to report, on an exclusive basis, the formidable results that were achieved.
Following the stirring opening address by the President of the Swiss Wine and Fondue Growers Association, the working committee devoted itself to the difficult task of determining how fondue should be advertised and marketed and how the various types could best be distinguished from one another. This, it was hoped, would prevent the confusion that occurs when a visitor to Switzerland orders a cheese *fondue* and receives

a *fondue bourguignonne* – cubes of beef cooked in oil – certainly no less tempting, but admittedly rather different in consistency. With such rampant chaos in the fabled land of peace and order, something obviously had to be done. And so it was decided to indicate clearly on every bill of fare in the country the intrinsic differences between cheese *fondue* and *fondue bourguignonne*.
No sooner had this admirable mission been accomplished – with the assistance of voluntary contributions from all over the world – than a rash of new and more fanciful *fondues* began appearing all over Switzerland. Now everything seemed hopeless and the committee faced the almost futile problem of differentiating between cheese *fondue*, *fondue bourguignonne*, *fondue orientale* and *fondue chinoise*, among others. Special letters were sent out to restaurateurs, cautioning them on the dangers of creating havoc with Switzerland's national dish, which should, everyone admitted, be protected under Swiss – if not international – law.
At the same time, a Library of Fondue Technique and Information (known as LOFTI) was established, so that all new varieties could be catalogued, with a specimen of each maintained at the Federal Bureau of Weights and Standards. With this herculean undertaking now a matter of official record, it is finally possible to advise the tour-

ist on what types of *fondue* are available to him. A brief sampling from the voluminous files of the Library of Fondue Technique and Information shows the following varieties as having been registered during the past thirty-one months:

Fondue suédoise
A tantalizing concoction of meatballs cooked in whale oil
Kosher fondue
Old-fashioned kreplach cooked before your eyes in genuine chicken fat
Fondue accidentale
House specialty, sometimes listed as *fondue surprise*
Fondue irlandaise
New potatoes cooked in boiling water

Many of the *fondue* dishes registered at the library are passing fads, of this there can be no doubt. But, through careful planning plus a high degree of intelligence and hard work, the Swiss people have succeeded in protecting their vested interests in the *fondue* industry. With the help of wise and courageous information services, visitors to Switzerland are now able to eat what they order in all 25 cantons of the country, including Alaska and Hawaii.

Cookiewasher

People often ask me how I, as an American, feel living in a country as small as Switzerland. First of all, it's somewhat fallacious to think of the country as being small, despite what the geography books may say and despite the innumerable – and sometimes even humorous – stories on the subject. Every student of Swiss-American relations knows that Switzerland is about three times the size of Connecticut or the equal of two Massachusettses, while others like to consider it half the size of Maine. Why all these comparisons are limited to the New England states is the subject of some conjecture among Americans living here, but the consensus has it that Connecticut and Massachusetts are two names even the Swiss cannot pronounce correctly, with Maine simply thrown in for good measure. This is perhaps unfair to the Swiss, for they are certainly the most gifted linguists one is likely to meet up with, their own Swiss-German language excepted, of course.

Swiss-German is unquestionably in a category of its own, but not everyone dislikes it immediately – some realize only later how strange it really is. I remember my first day in Switzerland, quite a few years ago. A friend had located a room for me in a small pension near the university in Zurich. That first day, at breakfast, a young man who was studying at the Swiss Federal Institute of Technology looked at me with sleepy eyes and asked me if I could pronounce the word "Chuchichäschtli". I replied that I was not acquainted with Arabic and hadn't come to Switzerland for any purpose other than seeing the country and learning German.

"That *is* German," my student friend countered, beaming a smile of victory mixed with strawberry jam. "Chuchichäschtli", he went on to explain, meant "kitchen cabinet" in Swiss, and it was a very important term. I disclaimed any interest in politics so early in the morning, and tried to change the subject by remarking how good the rolls and coffee were. He said that Swiss rolls were *always* good and that Americans, as far as he knew, were all as naïve as I. He added that "Chuchichäschtli" was *the* word, the absolute ultimate in words with which the Swiss plays his favorite game with Americans, a game called "Pronounce Me if You Can".

"Oh," I remarked, "please forgive my ignorance. Allow me to make a stab at your favorite word!" And out it came: "Xhruckiplaster!" His face turned pale, then beet red. He began shaking from the ankles to the top of his head, and soon he was bellowing out the most amused laughter I have ever heard. "Haw, Hew, Haw," he wheezed.

ch li li

Chu chi chä li

ch ch ch chu- chi- chä- li

Ch ch ch ch... li CH ch CHcH

CH ch ch ch

Ch ch ch Chu- chi- chä- Ku Ki Kä

Ch chu chi li chä chuchichäch

chchch li CHCHCH chchchch

chuchichächuch chchchchch Li

ch ch ch ch chä

CHu Chuchichä CH

CH Li CH Li

1st LESSON

"Chukeecaskly," I said hopefully, but his laughter only increased in intensity. I became panicky. "Custardcashly," I quickly offered. "Crashpervesply", "Cookiewasher", "Caspergustly", "Raspervestly". By now, three other house guests had entered and were quietly witnessing a scene they had probably observed at least ten times before. With a last desperate gasp, realizing that I was an unofficial representative of the United States of America in a foreign country, I sighed, "Chuchichäschtli".

Silence reigned over the breakfast room. Frau Böschli, our landlady, who was just bringing in a fresh pot of coffee, stopped and stared. What had I done, had I insulted one and all of them? Was there some Swiss custom – some quaint bit of etiquette – I had breached? Was I to be banished from this country which I was just beginning to like? My fears were quickly allayed when the student engineer, smiling from ear to ear and looking no worse for wear following his terrible attack of laughter, stood up and tipped an imaginary cap to me.

"Young man," he said, "you have passed the test with floating colors, as you say in America."

"What test?" I wanted to know.

"You have mastered the password, you have acquitted yourself with dignity and aplomb. You have become one of us, one of the noble breed who founded the Confoederatio Helvetica in the year 1291. To you, sir, our heartiest congratulations for having pronounced 'Chuchichäschtli' correctly – exactly as a Swiss would have."

I started to say that it was only an accident, but I realized that such an admission would have spoiled their entire day. "Thank you," I said instead, "I'm proud to be in Switzerland."

Frau Böschli, who hadn't uttered a word until now, said, "He speaks 'Chuchichäschtli' like a Basler – and they're not Swiss, not one of them is a Swiss!" "Basler or no Basler," said the man who had started the whole kitchen-cabinet business, "he's one of us, and we'll see to it that his Swiss education continues in the spirit in which it started."

I was glad to have made so lasting an impression upon these kind people, all of whom had been complete strangers only a few minutes earlier. "Chuchichäschtli" proved to be more than a password. It was evidence that I feared nothing in Switzerland, that I experienced no innate feeling of horror at the prospect of speaking Swiss-German.

I didn't know it then, so long ago in Frau Böschli's breakfast room. Switzerland, you see, is a small country in many ways that one would hardly suspect. It isn't small because it comprises only 15,950 square miles – three times the size of

Connecticut or the equal of two Massachusettses. It isn't small in that sense at all, for most of those square miles are up and down, and somebody once said that if you flattened out Switzerland with a rolling pin, it would be about the size of the Soviet Union. No, if Switzerland is small in any respect it's because of the fierce pride of her people, these descendants of the Helvetian tribes and the Roman legions. Unbeknownst to me, I had tickled that pride and catered to the Swiss desire to be liked, to be recognized for what they are. I had done all this – and it proved a valuable lesson for everything that would follow – by pronouncing one small word correctly. And in all the years that followed, I was never able to do it again.

James Blaisdell Wetherby

James Blaisdell Wetherby visited Switzerland for the first time just over one hundred years ago. It is therefore fitting that the gifted American poet and novelist now be accorded the recognition he so richly deserves in the country he loved so much.

The works of James Blaisdell Wetherby have been of considerable benefit to Switzerland, despite the fact that Wetherby himself – modest by nature – remains relatively unfamiliar. Yet we have all read, and profited from, the stirring words of his epic poem, *An Alptime Wonder*. But how many of us realize that, were it not for Wetherby's glowing description of the Val Bain-de-Mousse, this popular spa and winter resort might still be unknown today?

Wetherby came from a simple yet remarkable background. He grew up on the outskirts of Miskiwawa Junction, a former Iroquois settlement on Long Island. As a child, he spent hour upon hour studying the multicolored clamshells which the wildly tossing surf deposited on the fine white sand of the South Shore. On one of his excursions to the beach, Wetherby came upon a piece of driftwood with strange foreign markings on it. After careful examination, he was able to decipher the words: "Made in Switzerland –

Another Swiss Quality Product – For Export Only". The die was decidedly cast. Young James knew that the far-off country which had produced this driftwood must be fascinating, and from that time forward he was obsessed with the idea of visiting Europe – and Switzerland!
After the completion of his studies in England, James Blaisdell Wetherby's wish was fulfilled. He entered Switzerland on horseback, at Basel, having traveled from London via Paris and Troyes. Here an excerpt from his journal, dated May 14, 1865:
"This day we proceeded from Basel to Neuchâtel, a neat, orderly town at the foot of the Jura mountains and on the western shore of the lake which bears the same name as the town. If I could but describe to you the deep blue of these waters! Though the scene was as tranquil as any that had ever met my travel-weary eyes, I nevertheless felt a certain restlessness, for the purpose of my visit – to enter true alpine country – had yet to be accomplished. Far in the distance, in an easterly direction many leagues away, swathed in the pale mists, lay the ice-covered giants – the mountains of the Ober Land. I sensed their mysterious presence even though I could not always see them. I felt the inspiration they had bestowed on generations of writers before me. The day was crisp and pleasant, what one would expect of spring-

MADE IN
SWITZERLAND

time in Switzerland. A peasant maid, wearing her native costume, waved prettily and bid us *bonjour* as we made great haste towards Berne, seat of the Confederation, historical metropolis, gateway to the sleeping glacial eminences of the Ober Land."

Switzerland is proud of those artists and writers of the past who sought inspiration or refuge within her borders. For this reason, the Swiss National Council decided to publish a special commemorative set of Wetherby's works, including his Swiss Journal, the alpine poems and novels, and a critical essay, *What Will the Stormy Wetherby?*, by Gilfred Mascoach, F.B.I.

The first volume of the set contains Wetherby's best-known lines, inspired by Lord Byron and the Castle of Chillon. The poem is entitled *Le lac est beau et grand:*

Upon yon peak, O gold of Spring,
The Dent-du-Midi, let fantasy ring,
Without the rays of sun and shine,
What would it be, were it not thine?

The waters below, upon the Chillon,
Cast their spell – O vast carillon! –
Whose tones sound bold upon the old,
A noble story, never told.

Lac Léman, why must I leave thee?
Traveling on will never relieve me

Of thoughts enchanting, spun in silk,
How I crave this land of milk!

This was James Blaisdell Wetherby's literary greeting to Switzerland, a country he would learn to admire and understand even more as the years passed. Although he made several trips to America during the following three decades, Wetherby considered Switzerland his home. This was officially confirmed by the Cantonal Parliament of Appenzell, which granted Wetherby the first residence and work permit it had ever issued by official decree. The poet thanked his benefactors in characteristic style:

Had I but guessed that I, the guest,
Were blessed by test, in quest of rest,
The best of crests upon my vest
Caressed in nests along the West.

James Blaisdell Wetherby lived the greater part of his life in Switzerland. When he died, in 1899, there were few who remembered him, for he had spent his last years quite alone, studying mineralogy and glaciology on the Pfannenstiel, near Zurich. He told occasional visitors that this area reminded him of the Texas Panhandle, the subject of one of his earlier novels.

This unique poet, this titan among men, lived quietly and peacefully. His discovery that the thermal springs of the Val Bain-de-Mousse contained pure gold, in addition to sulphur, obviously contributed to the world-wide attraction of this spa. In fact, it was the first time in recent history that one could take the waters in an aura of wealth and other assorted minerals.

Switzerland owes a debt of gratitude to James Blaisdell Wetherby, one that will be paid when, on the two hundredth anniversary of the poet's first visit, a "Wetherby Year" will be proclaimed. In the meantime, interested readers may obtain the booklet, *James Blaisdell Wetherby – The Peregrinations of a Popular Poet*, now being prepared by the writer's granddaughter, Heidi Miskiwawa Wetherby.

Health and Schübligs

Some day, I shall seriously try to lead an unhealthy life in Switzerland. Not that I have anything against being healthy. As a matter of fact, before I came to this country, I had considered myself a fair specimen of American manhood. But I had much to learn.

I learned that living in Switzerland would restore my health to what it was before it began to falter. There were few noticeable symptoms, and I even felt quite well. I was occasionally tired, especially after having stayed up late the night before. And my appetite, once of legendary repute, was but a shadow of its former self, particularly after I had finished eating. What, then, was really wrong with me?

Whatever it was, said one of my new Swiss friends, I would have to undergo a "cure". This innocent word frightened me, and it conjured up visions of shock treatments and being strapped to a table. When my complexion had returned to its natural pallid color, my acquaintances explained that the cure they had in mind entailed no more than swimming in a thermal pool, of which there were many in Switzerland. I was grateful for their helpful advice. I was also relieved that my condition could be so easily diagnosed and so pleasantly treated.

"Tell me," I asked Walti, the ringleader of my health-cure friends, "when should I begin my cure and where do I go? Lastnotleast (I was proud of this Swiss expression), please give me all the other details I ought to know."
Walti looked puzzled. He turned to his wife, Ruthli, and then he looked back at me. Ruthli joined in the conversation by suggesting that I take the waters at Loèche-les-Bains, a spa in the Valais. "There," said Ruthli, "he will have the benefit of water that comes out of the earth at 51° centigrade. Furthermore, Loèche-les-Bains has hyperthermal gypsum springs with calcium and magnesium sulphate waters and strontium and fluorine waters – exactly what he needs!"
Walti seemed to agree. Then, raising his head and observing me more closely, he pointed out that my eyes had a very strange appearance, and that what I needed was sulphur – good, old-fashioned sulphur – to recondition the blood and to re-instill some old-fashioned sparkle in my tired, bloodshot eyes.
"Loèche-les-Bains is fine," he went on, "but if you really want sulphur, you must go to Schinznach Bad. Balneologically speaking, the sulphur spring at Schinznach produces water at 34° centigrade, hydrocarbonate waters with high hydrogen sulphide content, even slightly radioactive – very good for you – with low bromine and boric

acid content and some extremely active ions, too. Excellent for bringing back the appetite!"
I was already beginning to get hungry, and all the talk about water was making me thirsty. "I feel a little better now," I had to admit. "May I invite you fine people to join me in my favorite local inn?" We agreed to visit the nearby Gasthaus zum Kartoffelstock, which looks out towards the mountain of the same name.
There I immediately ordered a large, cold glass of beer and two of those wonderful Swiss sausages – *Schübligs* – which are almost as long as a full-grown dachshund.
"Wait!" said Walti and Ruthli in chorus. "Your health, remember."
"I'm hungry. I'm very, very hungry," I said almost tearfully, "and I want my *Schübligs* and my beer."
"Have them if you wish," offered Walti. "But if I were you, I'd order a camomile tea at 94° centigrade and a *Birchermüesli*."
My appetite suddenly and inexplicably disappeared. "I want a cold drink," I wailed, thinking that this might diminish the perspiration on my flushed forehead. "Anyway, what is a *Birchermüesli*?" I asked with bated breath.
Before the answer came, the waitress brought me a huge glass of brilliantly foaming beer – and the two *Schübligs*. I drank, lovingly and tenderly, sa-

voring the robust flavor of this fine Swiss brew. "Wait!" a voice shouted from across the room. I looked through the undulating layers of cigar smoke and saw an elderly gentleman, motioning for me to put the glass down. He then made his way over to me, holding his own glass of beer. "My," I thought, "aren't these the friendliest people in the world. Why, he just wants to drink to my health because I'm a stranger in these parts."

I raised my glass to him, and, in my very best German – learned on a two-day visit to Heidelberg – said "Ex!", which means "down the hatch". "No, no, you do not understand," he protested. "I only wanted to tell you not to drink that beer so cold – it's bad for the stomach – and I know that you Americans are always drinking ice-cold beverages."

Well, he was right – no argument there. And then he motioned to the waitress to bring me what he called a *Bierwärmer*, which is just about what it sounds like. The waitress returned with what looked like a divining rod, and she plunked it into my beautiful beer. After four minutes, I was told to remove the *Bierwärmer* and given permission to drink further. I removed it, burning my thumb and index finger in the process. The beer was now, as my friends exclaimed, at room temperature, and I need fear nothing more. I drank it.

MENU

Meanwhile, Ruthli and Walti were eating my *Schüblígs*, which I had forgotten in the confusion. "Too fattening for you," said Walti, "bad for the heart and the cholesterol count. We've ordered you a *Birchermüesli* with strawberries instead." When it arrived, I ate it – and it was quite good. But it wasn't a *Schüblig*.
Then I remembered something I had observed many times in restaurants all over Europe. "Fräulein," I addressed the waitress, "could you please bring me a little something for my dog ... he hasn't had enough to eat today."
"You have a doggie?" Walti asked. "What kind of doggie?"
"Oh, er, I have a ... a dachshund, a very long, lovely dachshund," I replied. "Fräulein," I continued, "please bring me two uncooked *Schübligs* for my dachshund, and put them on the bill."
Walti insisted on paying for everything, and, after I received the dog package from the waitress, we all left. As he got into his car, Walti reminded me to make a cup of camomile tea when I got home. I assured him that I would.
When I arrived home, I put a pot of water on the stove, took out the *Schübligs* and gently dropped them into the water. As they were slowly heating, I opened the icebox and viewed with joy the gleaming array of comestibles staring back at me. I grabbed the relish and the Dijon mustard, the

olives, the pickles, the mayonnaise, the cocktail onions, the horseradish and the piccalilli. Impatiently, my mouth watering, I waited for the *Schübligs* to reach a temperature of 94° centigrade.

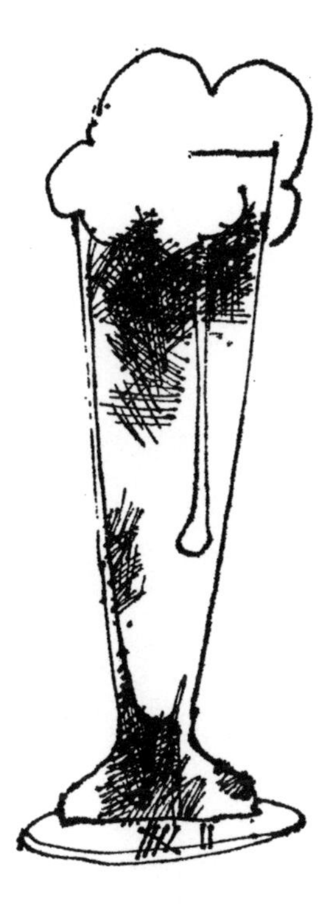

Say It in Swiss

Mark Twain seems to have slept in almost as many places in Europe as George Washington did in America. As a matter of fact, if one were to compute the number of hours the good humorist is supposed to have spent in various European resorts alone, one would find that he lived to the ripe age of three hundred and twenty-seven years. And when he wasn't sleeping in every hotel on every European byway, Mark Twain was creating aphorisms and local bits of humor, much of which is as valid today as when it was written.

In one particularly famous piece, he took apart the German language in such a devastating manner that it will probably never recover from the onslaught. Among other helpful suggestions to tourists, he pointed out that one can speak German quite acceptably with a vocabulary of but three magic words. The first of these was *Zug*, with a total of 544 different meanings (drawing, expedition, blast, railway train, flock, migration, platoon, inclination, etc.).

If this first attempt should fail to elicit an intelligent response, the next word to try was *Schlag*, with only 392 basic meanings, but far more colorful and more likely to be universally understood (punch, rhythm, carriage-door, tilled field, fit of apoplexy, etc.). Should fate nevertheless spare one the satisfaction of being understood with either *Zug* or *Schlag*, continued Mark Twain, the last resort was to stare your conversational opponent in the eye and say: "*Also!*" I may be misquoting the author of *A Tramp Abroad*, but this was, in any case, the general idea.

It's too bad that Mark Twain did not have a go at the Swiss-German language, for here he would have found a wealth of material at his disposal. But the subject is still virgin territory, with the exception of those well-known remarks comparing Swiss-German to a throat disease or some other illness. Nothing is further from my thoughts than to malign the most widely spoken language in Switzerland or to discuss expressiveness or musical values or whatever else passes for scientific evaluation of other people's native tongues. On the contrary, I want simply to offer my personal advice to those visitors who would like to get along in Swiss-German:

Grüezi

Most important word in Switzerland. Means, roughly, "Hi, neighbor", and is generally followed by a nod of the head and a very quick smile.

Grüezi mitenand

Same as above, except that *mitenand* means "all

together", hence "greetings, all together", when more than one person is present.

Guet Nacht mitenand

"Sleep well, all together."

Oder?

"Or?" Frequently used. May be substituted for the period in every Swiss sentence and is the first known instance of phonetic punctuation in a modern language. Means, "If you don't agree with what I'm saying, you can very well leave the premises." In American jargon, the equivalent phrase might be, "Wanna make something of it?"

So

Means almost anything, but used chiefly whenever a conversation seems to be slowing down to prove that the participants are not falling asleep. With great inflection, the combined form, *So-So*, may be repeated incessantly to mean, for example: "Last week while visiting my aunt in Winterthur I heard the most remarkable account of her trouble with the local plumber who insisted on dismantling the hot-water pipes while the children were in the bathtub but I told her not to worry that's one of the disadvantages of prosperity and the time will come again when these people will be happy when a few crumbs are tossed their way."

Ja-Ja

"I couldn't agree with you more." On certain occasions, natives of northern Switzerland can be overheard conversing in these unique short forms, of which every other modern country should be envious:

Fritzli:

(Entering a typical local inn in Switzerland) Grüezi, Ueli.

Ueli:

Grüezi, Fritzli.

Fritzli:

Ja-Ja.

Ueli:

So-So.

Fritzli:

Isch wahr (how true)! Oder?

Ueli:

Glaubsch (do you think so)? Oder?

Fritzli:

Ja-Ja.

Ueli:

So-So.

So much for our first lesson in the Swiss-German language. Now, to reduce what we have learned to the barest essentials, keep the following rules in mind:

1. If it says *Grüezi* first, say *Grüezi* back.

SOSO
JAJA
SOSO
JAJA
SOSO
JAJA
SOSO
JAJA
SOSO
JAJA

2. If it moves or seems alive, say *Grüezi* anyway.
3. If it doesn't move or seem alive, pick it up, and help keep Switzerland looking neat.

Those readers interested in furthering their knowledge of one of the world's most fascinating languages may write to the author, requesting a copy of the interesting booklet, *The Development and Derivation of Swiss-German from Its Earliest Known Beginnings in the Pleistocene Period to Its Present-Day Form and 93 Dialects*. This publication will be available for distribution as soon as the necessary research has been completed.

Switzerland Sings

Wherever one travels, it's a good thing to get close to the people, for this cements international relations, creates goodwill and plants the seeds of understanding in fertile ground for future harvest. And there is often no better way to get to know the people of a foreign nation than to learn their songs and dances, the heart and soul of any country. Switzerland is no exception to this rule, and it is always thrilling when a visitor is able to sing a local folk song. Imagine the pride of an American were he to hear a Swiss singing *Take Me Out to the Ball Game* or *Who Put the Overalls in Mrs. Murphy's Chowder?* By the same token, chills of something resembling emotion shoot up and down the Helvetic spine when a guest of the country joins in an old-fashioned Swiss community sing.

One of the most beautiful folk songs in Switzerland, conjuring up memories of an alpine paradise, is *Le vieux chalet*. It begins:

Là-haut, sur la montagne,
L'était un vieux chalet.
Murs blancs, toit de bardeaux,
Devant la porte, un vieux bouleau,
Là-haut, sur la montagne,
L'était un vieux chalet.

These touching lines, fraught with meaning, tell of a Swiss merchant's yearning to return to the mountains, where he has just remodeled an old chalet. The plaintive words describe his feelings when he first learns what the lovely old chalet will cost. Tears welling up inside him, he signs the contract and secures a building permit to enlarge the maid's quarters. No sooner does he start remodeling than the building contractor raises the price of paint and nails, and the merchant must take a loan to continue his project. *Le vieux chalet* is sung to the same melody as the well-known British folk song, *Yon Pye in the Skye*, so that there should be no difficulty for those who want to learn it.

Another typical Swiss song, from the Lake of Lucerne region, is the popular *Wind in My Chimney*, similar in melody to *Blow the Man Down*. *Wind in My Chimney* describes a Föhn storm in the mountains, and is one of the oldest songs in Switzerland. It had already fallen into obscurity when it was found on an illuminated manuscript in the dark and dusty recesses of the Cloister of San Giovanni in Golino (Canton of Ticino). The words themselves are based on the innermost feelings of a lonesome alphorn player, and they read as follows:

Holi-do-lee-do,
Holi-do-lee-day.

Holi-da-lee-da,
Holi-all-the-day.

One of the most attractive songs in the entire ethnic literature of Switzerland is *Vreneli, Vreneli, ich lieb dich.* Like so many songs of the early eighteenth century, it tells of a young Swiss lad and his love for Vreneli, daughter of a neighbor. Whatever he does, wherever he goes – down into the valley or into military service as a mercenary – our young Swiss thinks of his Vreneli. He imagines her sitting on her three-legged stool, milking the goats, Schwänli and Bärli. He hears her singing and begins to sing himself. He sings of his travels and his loves, and he always returns to the thought of Vreneli, his Vreneli! If only he had a picture of Vreneli, but the camera had not yet been invented. Alas! He must remember Vreneli as she was when he left her. Now, as he reaches into his pocket for his tobacco pouch, out falls a golden twenty-franc piece. Our mercenary studies the glittering coin – turning it over and over in his hand – and sees the face of Vreneli staring at him. He sees her beautiful golden hair and realizes again that he will always love his Vreneli. And this is why, even today, twenty-franc gold pieces are referred to as "Vrenelis". This is also why the Swiss have been known to fall in love with the coins in their pockets.

20
FR

Then there are the drinking songs! What gaiety, what laughter and good humor as the Swiss gather in their local inns to raise their voices and glasses on high. One song, *Let's Have Another* (Fräulein, no 's Bierli bitte), is extremely popular throughout German-speaking Switzerland. It is a traditional yodel in three parts, with an unusual syncopated rhythm reminiscent of the peasants of Appenzell, who learned this technique from the gypsies in the latter part of the seventeenth century. Although the texts of such songs are difficult to translate, we have secured an authentic version, found among the papers of Edward I. Lash, the famous British alpinist:

Let's have another, the evening's still young.
Why go home? We're here to have fun.
The inn's where we live, the home's where we sleep,
We only need to pay our keep.

Let's drink right now to every hausfrau
And to all the wives we know.
We're happiest here with good old Swiss beer,
Where women can't spoil the show.

Aces Are Low

For those who wish to delve into the eccentricities and idiosyncrasies of Swiss life, there is nothing more rewarding than to learn *Jass*, the Swiss national card game. In most countries, people play cards for want of something better to do. The Swiss, however, play almost as a profession, relegating other occupations to those times when it is impossible to round up a *Jass* foursome.

Jass is reputed to be one of the most relaxing games ever invented. I am more inclined to think that the participants relax from the murderous tension of the game only when it has ended, which it never seems to do.

Some months ago, I considered it high time to begin learning the intricacies of this age-old game. How could I hold up my head in Switzerland without knowing something of this important tradition? What would I do if, late at night, one of my Swiss acquaintances invited me to join a *Jass*-playing group? I would simply have to participate or be socially ostracized for the remainder of my stay in this interesting country.

And so, one evening, I met secretly with two old friends, Walti and Heiri, who were determined to initiate me into the solemn formalities of their favorite indoor sport. I say "secretly" because the Swiss themselves are intuitively aware of how to

Jass (they are apparently born with this knowledge), and how could I inform the population at large that I had stopped playing cards years earlier – when "casino" was *the* game in America? Even then I had been singularly untalented for this sort of thing.

Our *Jass*-learning session took place in the back room of the Gasthaus zum Kibitz, famous for its intercantonal *Jass* championships. We sat down and Heiri ordered the "tools", as he put it.

I was frightened. The light was dim and the look on the faces of my adversaries was determined. "What tools do you plan to use?" I croaked. The waitress then arrived with a small rug for the table, a pack of strange-looking cards, two pieces of chalk and a slate. I was informed that these were the tools of the *Jass* trade.

Now the evening began in earnest. Heiri flipped through the cards like a bored trans-Atlantic gambler. He asked me if I knew their names and those of the various suits.

"Of course," I replied. "Ace, king, queen, jack and all the rest. And everyone knows the suits: spades, hearts, diamonds, clubs, naturally." "No, my friend," said Heiri. "No such thing in Switzerland. You should know by this time that *everything* is different here. We have *Schilte*, *Schelle*, *Rose* and *Eichle*. And if your Swiss-German isn't good enough, this means 'shields', 'bells', 'roses' and 'acorns'."

This must be, I thought, the origin of the expression, "Large roses from little acorns grow." "So what do I do with the acorns, plant trees with bells on them?" I looked around to see how my humor had affected everyone.

"Listen," Walti said, "stop this funny business. *Jass* is serious, and if you want your residence permit renewed, you'd better learn it while you can. Opportunity doesn't knock *that* often."

And I learned and learned and learned. I learned on that evening and on many evenings that followed. I went to *Jass* clubs and *Jass* cellars, studied treatises on the subject written in the Middle Ages in Middle High German and took courses in memory improvement at the Federal Institute of Jass Technology.

My personal advice to beginners is to concentrate on learning the four suits – shields, bells, roses and acorns – then the cards themselves. Aces are high all over the world, but only sometimes in *Jass*. Here the jack, or "farmer", is high, followed by the *nell*, or nine. Then come the ace, the king and the queen. Only they don't call her a queen because women, until recently, were not permitted to play the game. As a matter of fact, as women become more and more emancipated in Switzerland, they begin to do things like playing *Jass*. First *Jass*, then – as we've already seen – they get the right to vote.

Jass vocabulary is quite unique. The queen is not really a queen because she not only looks like a he but is also seen smoking a pipe on two of the four suits, and a cigar on a third. She is called *Ober*, which means "over", and the jack, or farmer, is officially called *Under*, which means "under". The ten is under the under, but it's not called a ten because this would be too simple, and *Jass* is a complex game. The ten is a "banner" because that's what it looks like on the old cards. *Bock* means "high card" with various other connotations, while *Stich* (literally, "sting") means "trick".
When the game gets going, it resembles pinochle, which was probably derived from it. One suit is usually trump, except if somebody decides to play *Obenabe* or *Unnenufe*. This means top to bottom, starting with aces (and now they are high) or bottom to top, when sixes are high and aces low. Thus aces can be high, low or more or less in the middle. This would not in itself be so difficult, except it happens to everything in this incredible game. First high, then low, then worth nothing. Then worth everything. If you have a particular card at the beginning of a game, your partner will praise you for your cleverness. Later in the evening, you receive the same card and hold it for the psychologically perfect moment. You slam it on the table with a crack of your wrist. Your partner looks at you and calls you a

stupid *Löffel*, which means "spoon". Your opponents call you a *Jockelikopf*, which means "nincompoop". This is what happened to me at the Gasthaus zum Kibitz.

"Don't you remember," said Heiri, my partner and one-time best friend, "that a *Stöck* (marriage) and a *Drüblatt* (three-leaf clover) are worth twenty points? And you can certainly recall my telling you that in *Obenabe* or *Unnenufe* the score is

trebled and the eights count eight points each because the jack is no longer high but only worth two!"

"But I didn't realize we were playing *Obenabe* – I thought we were playing acorn trumps, or was it roses high with banners flying?"

"Acorn, schmaycorn," said Heiri, "you are no *Jass* player, that's what you aren't!"

"I'll try to improve, I swear it! Give me one last chance!" I begged.

"No. Finished, concluded, *aus*," everyone shouted at me. "From this day on," said Walti, "you may kibitz, but your playing days are over. Now turn in your cards and membership button and drink your beer."

But I was pleased with myself anyway. Think of all I had learned – how I had enriched my life with new and vital experience.

"*Jockelikopf*," I said to myself, "you're one lousy card player!"

Skiing Is Fun?

I don't enjoy skiing at all. This is because, for some inexplicable reason, I cannot take it seriously. A good skier should obviously *look* like a good skier – which disqualifies me from the start. I am incapable of curling up my lip or of creating that peculiar glint in my eyes that all good skiers seem to have. Of course I am a little envious of those who treat a gleaming slope as if it were Highway Number One from Boston to Bangor. This undoubtedly accounts for the difference in our personalities. To the ski enthusiast, that same slope represents a challenge to push on towards the unknown, a duel between man and nature, a clash of physical forces of unimaginable complexity.

When I stand at the top of such a slope – my feet imprisoned in safety bindings – and look down towards the distant valley, I usually begin laughing softly to myself. My laughter gradually increases in intensity until those around me notice it. Then, with a final "Ha-Ha" and "Ho-Ho", I push off with a flourish of ski poles and snow, slowly gathering speed until we – my skis and I – are smashing ahead at four miles per hour. I never had the impression that I was racing against the forces of nature or that there was any sort of clash of physical forces involved. I was simply too busy

trying to keep my balance. And, anyway, those wintry attacks of laughter were completely unpredictable and I never knew what the result might be.
Forty or forty-five yards down the slope I would invariably fall. It was always the same. My skis began moving at five miles per hour while I was still going four. The result was a clearly predictable separation of man and conveyance. I would fall – neatly and with artistic grace. The indentation left in the snow would have distinct and unmistakable lines, for I had made a study of how to fall and stay alive. According to my analyst, this is why I have to laugh as I stand so omnipotently on top of the slope.
Subconsciously I know that I shall fall – I have always known it – and I have made an art of it. Falling has become my means of showing my prowess on – or off – skis. A good skier may be a good skier, but he is almost always a bad faller. I am a bad skier but a good faller. I have never broken a bone since developing my personal falling technique, while good skiers continue to break their bones as if they grew on trees.
It started some years ago with my first ski lesson in Switzerland. I had entered the beginners' class of the ski school at an Engadine village where we were spending our winter holidays. I had no great desire to ski, even then. But my wife was

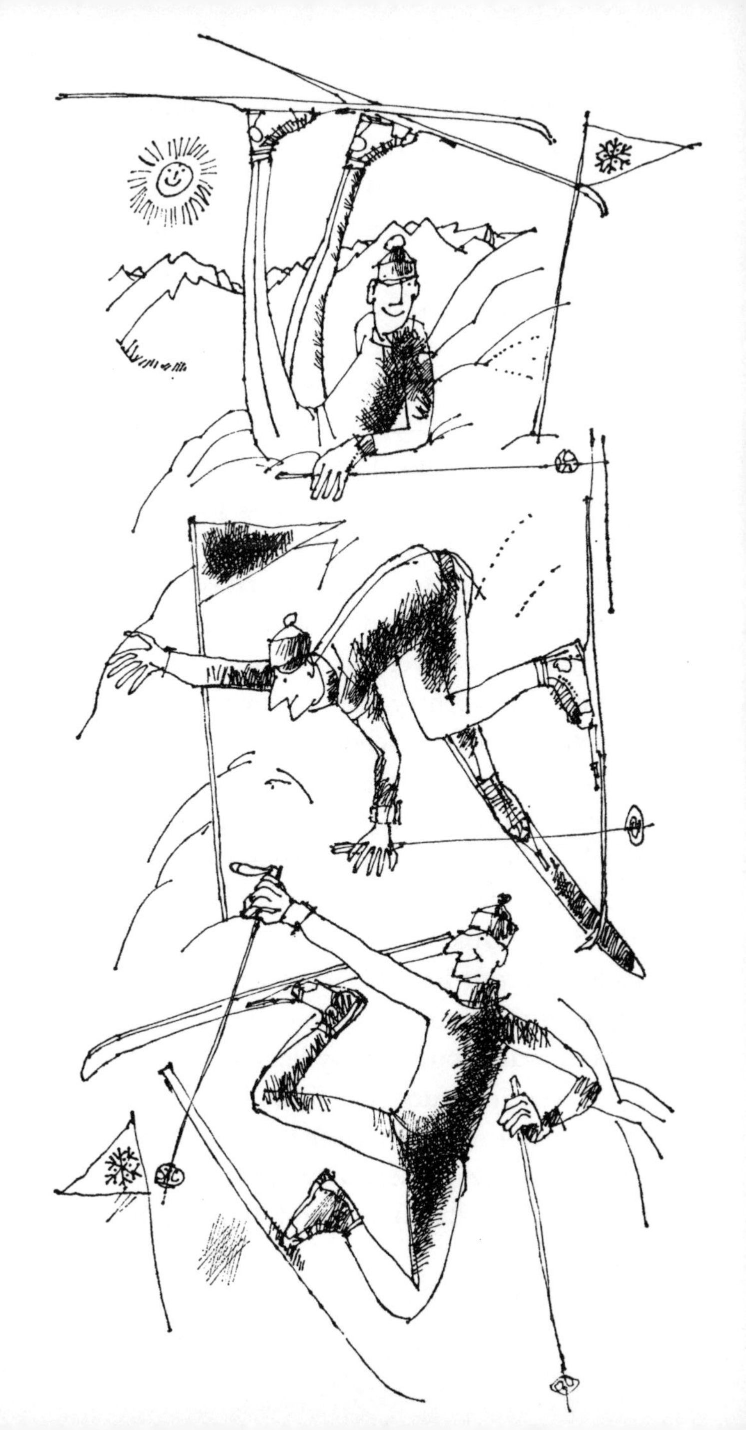

reasonably good – and so were my children – and I literally felt left out in the cold while they seemed to be having so marvelous a time. At first I fought the inclination to try. I fought it when it became a mild wish and I fought it some more when it became an irresistible compulsion. How nice it would have been just to sit somewhere – perhaps with a warming drink in my hands – and meditate. But my days of meditation were over. I had no further choice. I was caught up in the wiles and whims of my own ungrateful psyche.
And so I rented a pair of skis, as well as poles, boots and gloves, ski pants, jacket, goggles, straps, an altimeter and a compass. I bought the best and fastest silver wax available and, at eight o'clock one morning, set out for the beginners' class at the local ski school.
Swiss ski instructors are quite unusual. My teacher was named Reto (pronounced "ray-tow"), which I thought was a charming and colorful name until I learned that all ski teachers in Switzerland are named Reto. The Swiss manage to distinguish one Reto from the other by appending descriptive adjectives to each. For example, my Reto was known in the village as Young Reto. There were, of course, an Old and a Skinny Reto, a Farmer Reto (with fourteen cows) and a Farmer Reto (with three). There were Carpenter Reto and Plumber Reto, Radio Reto and Railroad Reto.

Young Reto introduced himself to me and the other members of the class. I was the oldest (the others ranged in age from six to eight), and Reto therefore asked me to lead off the various exercises which were designed to make professional skiers of us before the winter was over. We started with an elementary method of movement called "sliding and walking on the level". Basically, this means placing one ski before the other and simply moving. I led off and fell. The other nine members of my class followed – and each fell exactly where I did.

Young Reto rushed over and explained to my fellow pupils that they were to follow *him*, not me. They then proceeded to walk and slide on the level without incident. By that time I had untangled myself from my skis and had rejoined Reto and the class.

We then learned how to turn. First came an extremely easy form which I soon mastered. Then Reto showed us the Kick Turn and two or three other murderous operations which made me wonder if the whole thing was worth it.

"Listen," I said to Reto, "skiing really must be a fairly straightforward business, and I see no earthly reason to overcomplicate it."

Reto told me to keep quiet and pay attention as he continued to run through his repertoire of ski techniques. With each exercise, he seemed to be-

come more and more elegant. He jumped and turned with enormous ease. He skipped and swished wherever and whenever he wanted. And he never fell – not even once.
At the end of our second week, Reto announced that, if we wished, we could all take the Bronze Test. Those who succeeded in this qualifying test would be awarded a Bronze Medal. We could continue to improve each year and eventually try the Silver and Gold Tests.
We all entered the Bronze Test that next Friday. The entire class passed without difficulty – all except me. Reto was most sympathetic. He said he was sorry I hadn't passed, for it really wasn't that difficult. I interjected that I had certainly skied well, had I not? Yes, said Reto, but he mentioned that I had fallen in the middle or at the end of each exercise, and this had never happened before.
When they handed out the medals at the local inn, and each pupil was called to receive his, they waited until the end to mention my name. Reto stood up and announced a special award. The tension was great and there was a sudden, expectant silence in the audience. I rose and stood next to Reto, for I knew that my moment had come.
"Ladies and gentlemen," said Reto, "this evening you have witnessed the awarding of Bronze, Silver and Gold Medals. Tonight, for the first

time in the history of our ski school, we have the honor of presenting a new award. To this gentleman here, we now give our Tin Medal for outstanding performance in the difficult art of falling."

He pinned the handsome medal on my proud breast and kissed me on both cheeks. The audience cheered – and I began to laugh softly to myself.

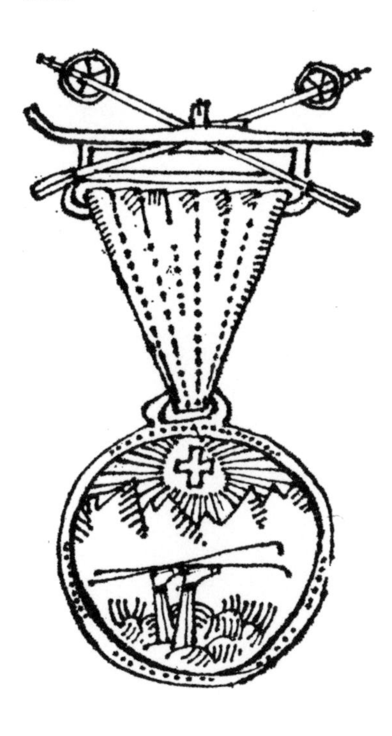

Letters to the Editor

Every so often, we devote space to questions asked by our readers. It is our hope, in this way, to encourage greater understanding of Switzerland's unusual situation in the world of today, and to contribute whatever we can to the international exchange of incongruous information. The following letters represent a small selection from those received. They were chosen primarily because the topics discussed were considered to be of great interest to our general readership.

Sir: My friends and I here in Wampum, Washington, are deeply fascinated by the saga of William Tell and the apple this famous Swiss hero shot off his son's cranium. Since Wampum is the apple-growing capital of America, we would appreciate some additional details on this historic event as it might apply to the apple-growing industry. We would especially like to know what variety of apple Mr. Tell used for his experiment, and whether it was red, green or yellow.

W.T., WAMPUM, WASH.

Apples have always been popular in Switzerland, even before William Tell chose to immortalize the health-giving fruit. The Romans were extremely partial to apples as far back as 44 B.C., when they founded Augusta Raurica near today's Basel. Tell's apple, a fruit of the rosaceous tree

Malus pumila, was selected for its perfect shape, its white meat and its worm-free exterior. Many years were to pass, however, before this particular apple was given the name *Tellus typus*, which is still in common use.

When the arrow from Tell's crossbow smashed through the *Tellus typus*, seeds from this prolific variety were scattered in every direction. Today, there are 7,434,000 apple trees in Switzerland, nearly all of which can trace their roots back to William Tell's fortunate shot. This is also where the expression "family tree" originated, for had it not been for an apple tree, William Tell's family, and perhaps the whole country, could not have existed. A grateful Switzerland has commemorated its national hero in many ways, particularly in its world-famous hotells and its tellephone system. In reply to the second part of your question, Tell's apple was bright red, a fact which should not be overlooked, for it undoubtedly helped him to aim in the right direction.

Sir: I am a housewife in Waukietaukie, Wyoming, and am also editor of the Waukietaukie Women's World. The topic at next month's meeting of our social club is "Switzerland, Tiny Democracy in the Heartland of Europe". As I am expected to moderate this meeting, I wonder if you can tell me everything about lovely Switzerland.

R. W., Waukietaukie, Wyo.

Certainly. Switzerland covers an area of 41,287.9 square kilometers, and is 220.1 kilometers wide at its longest north-south point, 348.38 kilometers long at its widest west-east point. Its highest point is the top of the Dufourspitze (4634 meters), its lowest the surface of Lago Maggiore (193 meters). The country's largest city is Zurich. Its smallest community is Illens, Canton of Fribourg, which has eleven inhabitants. (Zurich is considerably larger.) The Canton of Ticino entered the Swiss Confederation in 1803, while Valais, Neuchâtel and Geneva did not join until 1815. Uri, Schwyz and Unterwalden *formed* the Confederation in 1291. There were only 400 donkeys living in Switzerland in 1961, as opposed to 1600 in 1911, but, at the same time, there are now 75,000 ducks and geese. Duck figures are not available for the year 1911, since the first duck census did not take place until 1936. Ducks very much like Switzerland, mainly because of the many freshwater lakes, which are considered especially ducky. In 1936, somebody counted 1484 natural lakes in Switzerland, which then made it relatively easy to count the ducks swimming in them.

Sir: The question of language in Switzerland has always interested me. Here at home we speak only one language and we still have difficulty making ourselves understood

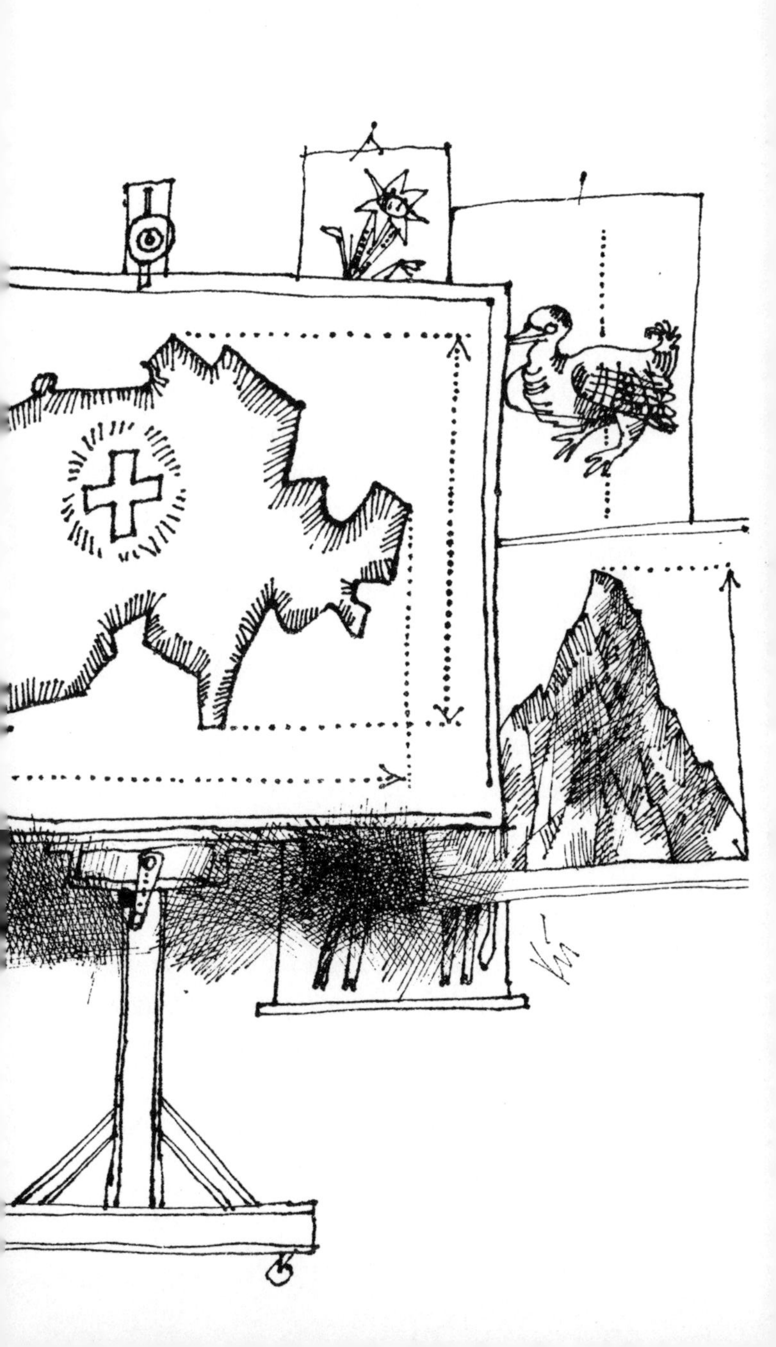

and getting things done. How is it possible that Switzerland, with four official languages, has learned to live with this problem?

P.R., LONDON, ENG.

In countries with a single national language, it can be insulting to assert that you do not understand what is being asked of you. In Switzerland, on the other hand, it is considered polite to say you do not understand, whether you do or not. To simplify this point, in Switzerland one need only understand what one chooses to understand. This is the same situation as exists in your country, only more diplomatic, and it is one aspect of the character which has made the Swiss so renowned for their diplomatic proclivities. It is also why Switzerland is so often the arbiter of international problems. In any case, if you really want to be understood in Switzerland, speak English. Everybody either speaks it or would like to speak it, and they will pretend to understand you, whether they do or not. I hope this is clear.

Sir: Some months ago, I read your article on the great American poet and novelist, James Blaisdell Wetherby, and I was impressed with his writings on Switzerland. Could you please tell me what you consider Wetherby's finest work?

M.E., MISKIWAWA JUNCTION, N.Y.

James Blaisdell Wetherby was one of the towering literary geniuses of his time: an American who not only lived in a foreign country, but also a person who was able to capture in words the feeling and heartbeat of that country. He chose Switzerland, and generations of students of the alpine country will be forever grateful for that fact. It is virtually impossible to single out his best work, for he was a productive writer of the highest literary quality. One essay found on the back of an old envelope three years ago is perhaps most typical of what Wetherby was trying to say. It is entitled *The Apple*, and it includes the memorable lines:

"Apples have always been popular in Switzerland, even before William Tell chose to immortalize the health-giving fruit. . . . Tell's apple, a fruit of the rosaceous tree *Malus pumila*, was selected for its perfect shape, its white meat and its worm-free exterior."

On Learning German

Some years ago, when I first came to Switzerland, the first thing I wanted to do was learn the local language. It hardly fitted into my scheme of things when I discovered that any number of languages and their respective dialects are spoken in this small country. All right, I thought, I shall have to start where I am. I'll have to learn German, for, after all, I was living in Zurich.

One day at breakfast in the small pension where I was living, I expressed this wish to the others at the table.

"German?" asked the student engineer whose favorite food was strawberry jam. "Why German? I mean, it is a related tongue – no doubt – but you should really learn *Swiss*-German, which is much older than German and more expressive, too."

"Good," I replied, "I shall be pleased to learn your Swiss-German, if you recommend it."

Frau Böschli, our landlady, who was just bringing a fresh pot of strawberry jam for the engineer, interrupted. "No one can *learn* Swiss," she said. "You must be born here to speak it correctly!"

"I'm frightfully sorry about the omission," I countered, warming up to the repartee, "but I've already been born – some years ago, on Long Island, State of New York."

Strawberries flew through the air as my student friend coughed out his last bite of roll with jam. Frau Böschli looked at her tablecloth – which had already been changed that month – and glared at me, as if I were responsible for the stains she would have to wash out. At the last moment she must have realized that I was a foreign visitor to her country, and she tried to be helpful.

"I honestly think you should start with the German language – just to build up a background, and then you can slowly acquire a genuine Swiss accent and all the rest. Anyway, you don't know if you're going to stay in our country *that* long. To begin with, why don't you go to the cinema every night – they show fine American and British films in Zurich – and read the subtitles? When somebody says something, you quickly read it underneath. Soon you'll be speaking like a native!" The others seemed to agree with her.

I took Frau Böschli's advice and went downtown that same evening. The film I chose to see was called "Prairie Dust", a classic known in German as "Der Schmutz der Prärie". I was learning already, and the film hadn't even started. When it did, I realized that Frau Böschli's suggestion had been a good one.

"I'll shoot ya dead, wise guy," said the hero at the beginning of the first reel. My eyes focused on the subtitle: "Ich schiesse Sie tot, Mensch."

Wonderful, I thought, what a way to learn a language! Just then two little boys appeared on the screen, playing cowboys and Indians. "Bang! Bang!" they said in unison. "Peng! Peng!" said the subtitle.

Then Daisy Mae, everybody's little darling of the Prairie Saloon, appeared. She waddled as gracefully as she could through the swinging doors and sat down at a table. "Gimme a whiskey, Sam," said Daisy Mae. My eyes dropped to the subtitles floating seductively over her ankles: "Gib mir einen Schuss Whiskey, Sam."

Two wicked-looking men in black entered. "Drop that gun, partner," one of them shouted to Sam the Bartender ("Lass deinen Revolver fallen, Partner,"). "O.K. ("Jawohl") ... but please ("aber bitte") ... don't shoot ("nicht schiessen")," implored Sam.

That was the extent of what I learned that night, for everything else was in English anyway. I mean cowboy was cowboy, gun was revolver, prairie was prärie, whiskey was whiskey. The only real difference I discerned was that bang was "peng" – and that made the evening worthwhile.

When I reported my findings to the breakfast-table assemblage the next morning, everyone was impressed. "You've learned your first lesson well," said Mr. Strawberry Jam (I never learned his real name). "But why spend all your money

on the movies? Just listen to the radio. It may sound like gibberish at first, but pretty soon you'll begin picking out words, then phrases, then whole sentences. It can't fail!"

I was a good student and a polite visitor to Switzerland, and I took his advice. That night I listened to what must have been a very important football match (we say "soccer" in America), while the student engineer recorded the whole thing on tape so that I could check the words later. "Who's playing?" I asked.

"The Grasshoppers are playing the All-Stars," he replied. I listened to the announcer describe the game, which sounded something like this:

"Die Teams are both gut, aber der Manager von der Grasshoppers ist besser. Die All-Stars are ein very fair Team wenn they are not handicapiert. Ach, dere ist ein offside Goal, aber no Score, nur ein Penálty. Himmel, what ein Match today!"

So I learned, when the evening was over, that match is match, team is team, and manager is manager. I absorbed new words like penálty and handicapiert, increased my vocabulary with Grasshoppers and *Fussball.*

The following morning I astounded everyone at the table with my first words of genuine High German. Goethe would have been proud of me. As Frau Böschli entered with the *Milchkaffee*, I bowed in her direction and said, "Guten Morgen, honey, was ist der Score today?"

"Have a roll and some jam," whispered the engineer, "and keep your mouth shut!"

"I would much rather a whiskey have," said I, pleased with my first inverted sentence. "But that comes first later, when I into the city shall go."

"Stop him, he's mad!" shouted Frau Böschli.

"It must be the weather," said the strawberry engineer. "What can we do with him?"

"Let your revolvers fall before I fall you all, you hear?" I noticed how the power of my German vocabulary had hypnotized everyone. They were startled, electrified and, of course, a little jealous too.

I got up from the table, proud of having acquired so much knowledge in so short a time. "Peng! Peng!" I snapped as I strode out of the room.

Climbing the Geiger

Most people know that there are a lot of mountains in Switzerland. In point of fact, there is at least one peak for each inhabitant of the country, with as many shapes and sizes as can be imagined. This means that everyone can have his private mountain, just as people in other countries have their private islands.

Mountains are, of course, larger than people, so that they are able to accommodate more than one person at a time. Consequently, one can choose almost any mountain – anywhere in the country – and proceed to sit on it, look at it, climb it or get inspired by it. Since it is difficult to move mountains in the literal sense, they also offer a high degree of security to the harried city-dweller caught up in the complexities of modern living.

Because each mountain has its own distinct appearance – one might say, its alpine personality – it has been given its own special name, too, a name frequently inspired by the shape of the peak or by the emotions produced. My favorite mountain, the one I was determined to climb, is called the Geiger, which, when translated, means the Violinist. The North Face of the Geiger was, in fact, never scaled before my first attempt, which was to take place in the dead of winter.

There is an old legend concerning the Geiger

which fascinated me from the beginning, probably because of my musical background. It tells of eerie, spectral sounds emanating from the menacing North Face. Cowherds in the valley below were entranced by this ethereal music, which they believed was produced by an old fiddler who made his home in the rocky crevices of the heights. When the Geiger music sounded, villagers were drawn by a strange magnetic force to the base of the mountain, where, when they looked up, they imagined they saw the violinist himself. Many accounts were written of this phenomenon in the early nineteenth century, including a well-known poem, *Fiddler on the Mountain:*

What form of music hear I here,
What does all this connote?
Who is this being up above,
Why does he play his note?

O Paganini of the hills,
Both king and queenie of the trills,
Play on and on and never stop
Until we reach you at the top!

The attraction of the old fiddler encouraged many alpinists before me to attempt the North Face. But it remained impenetrable, as mysterious and enigmatic as the music itself.

The story, as I've said, always fascinated me,

which is why I was determined to have a go at the North Face. Since even the most experienced climbers were obviously incapable of reaching the top, I logically felt that my lack of knowledge might well produce a successful result.
And so, one day when the winter sun shone brilliantly, I put on my mountain sneakers and rucksack and called the local TV station to inform them of my plans. I asked them please not to send a helicopter to follow my ascent, because I didn't want the noise to frighten away the old violinist, whom I wanted to interview on behalf of the newspaper *Tell*. I recalled the motto of this journal, "*Tell* tells all," and I wanted to give them exclusive rights to my unusual story.
When I arrived at the Little Fried Egg, at the foot of the Geiger, a crowd had already gathered. Mountain people seem to have extrasensory perception, for how else could they have known that I was planning my fearless ascent for this very day? I looked around me and saw a man who was renting out telescopes to the tourists, so that they could observe my climb. Other people were munching sausages and bread, which were being sold everywhere. A yodel group from the neighboring village of Lautersingen had come in a chartered postal bus to send me off with song. To the left of my starting point, a group of mountaineers – I recognized two or three of them –

were betting among themselves that I would not be successful.

"I'll show them all," I swore to myself. "Wait and see," I muttered under my breath. "An American will finally conquer your Geiger North Face with its overhangs and chimneys, its ledges and edelweiss. This ascent will go down in history, just as the story of Everest will never rest." Glaring disdainfully as I made my way through the sausage stands, I entered the wall, exuding confidence all the way.

I must admit that it was more difficult than I had thought. But, where a more experienced climber would have faltered, I threw caution to the alpine winds. I hammered hooks and spikes into the Geiger granite as if it were plywood, pulled myself onward and upward with brute force and sheer courage. Soon I reached the final overhang, an awesome roof of wind-blown rock – the only remaining hindrance separating me from the peak and victory! I clenched my teeth, took out my ice pick and rope, and climbed on – first straight up, then upside down, then around... and over. Just one more step, one more breath, one more minute ...

A helicopter had appeared, and a photographer, hanging perilously from a cable beneath it, was filming the final stages of my courageous ascent. I looked down. Far below I saw Swiss and American flags being waved by the eager spectators, who were following my every step with their rented telescopes.

Then I looked up. There… there, almost within my grasp, was the elusive peak. Suddenly I heard the strange music of the old violinist and I knew that the legend was true. Soon I would be witnessing a sight no man had ever seen before.

(To be continued)

A Lesson in Geography

During the recent annual congress of IMAGE (International Mission Advocating a Gorgeous Europe), the Swiss delegation submitted an interesting and rather startling resolution. In presenting the details, the chief Swiss delegate, Adalbert Spargel, announced that we must all be aware of one fundamental fact. "The image of Switzerland outside the country does not reflect all that we want it to be," said Mr. Spargel. "It may be an accurate image, but it is obviously not an authentically Swiss image." He continued:
"We may, on occasion, deplore – or adore – the attitudes and idiosyncrasies of our countrymen, or we may not, as the case may be. But we must be certain, at all times and in all ways, that the name and honor of Switzerland are maintained in every crook and nanny of this world, wherever there are men and women who can read. My delegation has therefore charged me to propose that a serious effort be made to mention something genuinely Swiss – at least twice in every sentence – in every document and newspaper story, in all advertising copy and slogans, in all books and periodicals.
"We further propose that, whenever possible, a Swiss village or town be mentioned – whether in context or not – and that these words be empha-

sized through the use of cursive, or *italic*, type." The proposal was greeted with mixed feelings. Amid shouts of "impossible", "unwarranted", "wonderful" and "insane", the Swiss delegation held its ground. The Printers' Union of Switzerland calmly announced that it was ordering a two-year supply of italics from the Monotype Corporation. The Federal Historical Association undertook a preliminary study of town and village names, coming to the conclusion that such a proposal was good but impractical.

Adalbert Spargel, himself the publisher of a leading Swiss newspaper, announced that his journal would be the first to adhere to the conditions of the new resolution. Two days later, the following headline appeared in his paper, the *Neue Basler Bratwurst*:

Grandson Grabs Gals, Says Court

On page six of the same edition, readers found these stories:

Castro at *Root* of *Misery*
Champagne Sales Harder, Crusch Apples
Laura Nods to *Fellers, Moron* in *Brig*

Little did the unsuspecting readers of the *Neue Basler Bratwurst* realize it, but Mr. Spargel had cleverly inserted the names of eighteen Swiss towns in these headlines, and had proved, once for all, that it could be done. Now, other villages began vying for the honor of being represented in the *Neue Basler Bratwurst* and in the many other newspapers which began making use of the Spargel technique (*Spargelzeit*, in German), as it came to be known. Soon, all of Switzerland was swept up in a frenzy of word games, and the original resolution – which seemed so absurd at first – was actually ratified and put into effect. Those people who wrote letters to newspaper editors also made use of the now-popular technique, in the hope that their hidden writing talents would be discovered by at least one publisher. Telephone and telegraph offices all over the country were swamped by callers seeking information on villages whose names might lend themselves for future use. All English correspondence sent out of Switzerland was required, according to the resolution, to have at least two such names in each sentence, as were the broadcasts of the Swiss Short Wave Service.

Almost everyone hoped that the more out-of-the-way places in Switzerland would thus come to the attention of the prospective tourist. And there were soon definite signs that the new system was producing results abroad, especially in Australia. The Swiss Federal Office for the Inculcation of Tourists published a brochure with the following text:

"In the Anglo-*Saxon* world, *rain* is not unknown.

But in Switzerland, where the weather is the *envy* of the world, you will be *schmitten hard*. From your *first egg* in the morning until your last *filet* at night, Switzerland is prepared to offer you not only a small fling, but a real, old-fashioned *diepflingen*. Remember, there is no *misery* in this lucky country. There are Swiss *gais* and *gals* just like yourselves, and you can meet them any evening in a lovely Swiss *taverne*, having *grub* or drinking *gingins* and tonictonics. To be *concise*, this is all according to the *motto*, 'Switzerland is a *Grand-event!*' Switzerland is the *envy* of everyone, this is why we like to blow our *horn*, in the hope that we shall be heard by young and old, *ins* and outs, by every *feller*, *moron* or *sage* – in short, by all those whose *yens* do not include the *Orient*. So, no matter how you measure this country, a *landquart* is as good as a landmile. Take full advantage of everything from *apples* to *champagne*, and there's always an interesting *curio* to be sent home to the *missy*. Take your pen right now, dip it into your *inkwil* and write to us – you'll never *rue* the *day*. Soon you will personally be saying *hallau* to Switzerland for the *first* time!"

An Arab sheik happened to read the above text shortly after it was published, and, following the exhortation, hastened to write to the Swiss Federal Office for the Inculcation of Tourists. Shortly thereafter, he flew from Bahrein to Zurich and began looking for the towns he claimed had originally been settled by his ancestors. The Swiss to whom he posed his questions were confused at first, but soon he found his way.

"Allah be praised!" he shouted, as he located the towns on a map of Switzerland. "They're still here, just as great-grandfather said they were. There's Malapalud and Agasul, and over here are Tolochenaz, Ftan, Sfazù and Pagig. And look, I've found Faoug, Aeuja, Azmoos, Fajauna and Stierva. Oh, Allah be praised! Wonderful country, Switzerland!"

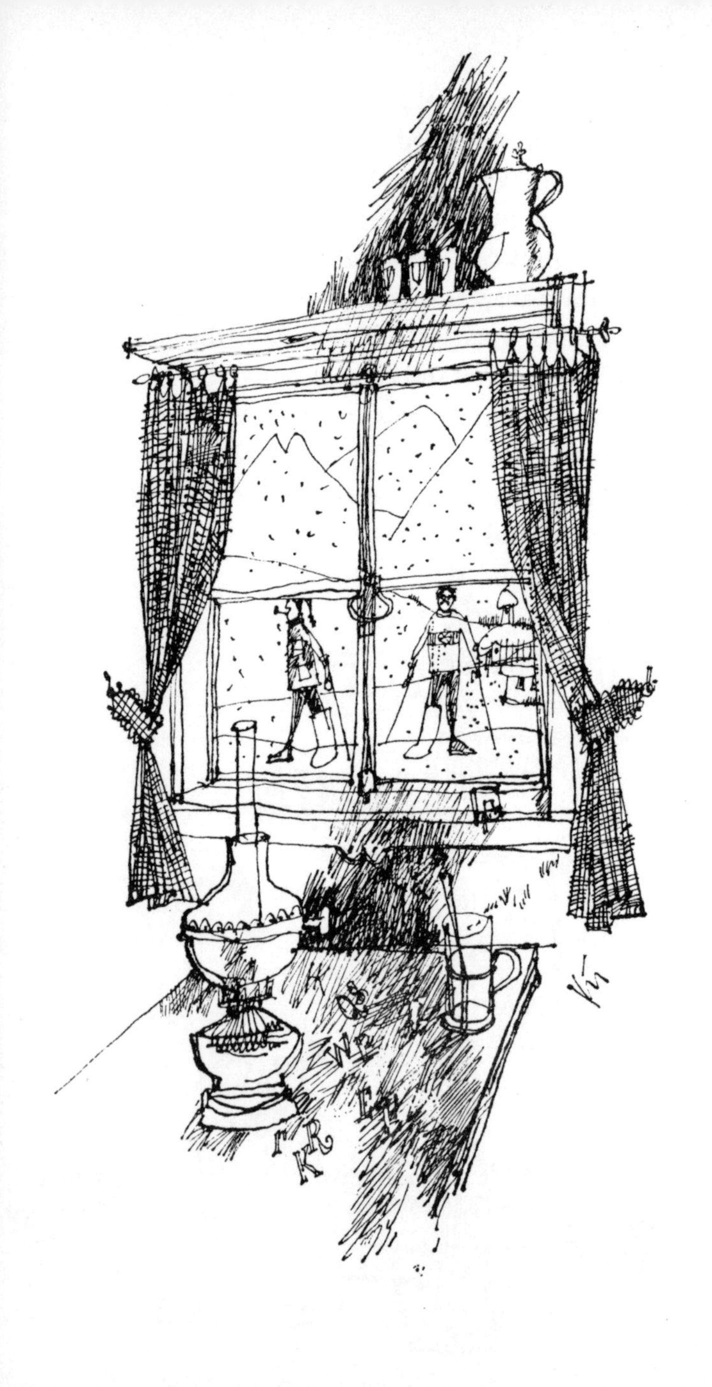

How to Ski Like Me

I'm really not much of a skier, and I therefore spend a great deal of my time explaining to everyone why I don't ski, why I cannot ski even if I wanted to and why I go to the foremost alpine resorts every year if I don't intend to. Basically, *not* skiing in Switzerland is quite a bit more difficult than giving in to the sometimes irrepressible urge to try. If you've ever heard a four-year-old child speak French and think that you ought to manage that language equally well, imagine the feeling of despair to see that same child gracefully shooting down the slopes on skis. And as you clumsily step aside to let him pass, you hear his "mer-ci mon-si-e-u-r" trailing off into the distance. By this time you're rather certain that the child in question is really more than an ordinary four-year-old. No, to comfort your injured pride – your *doubly* injured pride – you convince yourself that he must be something special, a future Olympic champion at the very least. So you decide that a reasonably mature American male ought to do just as well, and you make the fatal decision to try once more.

You rent a pair of skis – the best available – and set out towards the local *Idiotenwiese*, or "meadow of the idiots", for reasons which should be obvious to any skier. I don't know which is more difficult – walking with skis on your shoulders, precariously balanced on crossed ski poles, or walking with skis on your feet. Both methods are surely the product of a perverse sense of humor, for neither of them work and neither seems to be simpler than walking without skis in the first place.

Skiing, as I've indicated, is a tiring sport, and when you finally arrive at the beginners' slope you are already weary, both of the whole business as well as physically. Any good ski instructor – and there are hundreds in Switzerland – will warn you of the dangers of overexertion, so you decide to drop into the nearby ski hut before pressing on into the white wilderness.

Ski huts are a tradition throughout the Alps – they are informal and rustic, and they offer the exhausted skier a bit of nourishment when he needs it most. Needing it most after the 150-yard overland trek from my hotel, I sat down on a wooden bench and began to study the generations and generations of carved initials on the table before me. As I was contemplating these unique designs, a waitress appeared and asked what I wanted.

"Something hot," I replied.

"Coffee, tea, Ovomaltine or grog?" she asked.

Grog, I thought, would frighten away all remaining inhibitions, so I ordered one – with rum.

And there I sat, peering out at the omnipresent mountains through a window framed in calico. Romantic – no doubt of it – and the grog, welling up inside me, added to the atmosphere. The sun was brilliant on the shimmering snow as hundreds of skiers on the surrounding *pistes* came rushing down towards the village.

It was all so exhilarating that I had no choice but to motion to the waitress for another grog. I reveled in my new discovery; nothing enhances a day of skiing quite as much as grog sipped in the glow and warmth of a Swiss log cabin. I dreamt somewhat wistfully of attacking the ski runs at the 3000-meter level, of racing past row upon row of admiring onlookers – down, down, over the rocks, between the trees, fighting my spirited way ahead with deft movements of my hips and my ski poles. Now or never, I mused, and I paid and left the *Skihütte*, convinced of my own superiority.

As I started out towards the nearest chair lift, I wondered why I had never seriously considered becoming a ski instructor. How much I would enjoy living in such a village forever! There was the butcher shop, its window bulging with sausages and hams, and I walked on past the bakery with its *pâtisserie* and accompanying aroma of warm bread mixed with mountain air.

Then came the office of the village doctor, with

its neatly lettered sign: "Dr. Armin Legge, Spezialarzt für Hals- und Beinbruch". It was at that moment that I first noticed the parade of men and women on crutches going in and out of that village doctor's office. No, I thought – not that I'm afraid of a broken leg or two – after all, they are a badge of honor that good skiers wear with pride. But perhaps Dr. Legge has no time for me today. He *does* seem busy, just look at all his patients. Tomorrow is soon enough to start, I concluded. Unconsciously, I turned back from where I had come. Past the doctor's office, past the bakery and the butcher shop – *all* with neatly lettered signs – and into the *Skihütte*. In the door and back to my table with its generations of carved initials. "One grog, please," I said, as I settled down for the afternoon in my new-found home in the mountains of Switzerland.

Musical Inspiration

As far as anyone knows, the composer Karl Ditters von Dittersdorf never visited Switzerland. This fact is of some interest to musicologists, for Dittersdorf made use of alpine themes at least once or twice during his lifetime. The yodel chorus in Dittersdorf's operetta *Hieronymus Knicker*, written in 1787, was clearly inspired by an alphorn of the Bernese Oberland, for it was only here that the raised, or augmented, fourth tone was commonly used.

Dittersdorf himself was reluctant to discuss Switzerland, since he obviously did not want his contemporaries to learn how inspiring the country could be to anyone who wanted to write music. He took a special interest in the yodel form, particularly as it existed in the area south of Winterthur. Although he never heard the true alpine yodel – as Brahms later did – it is obvious that Dittersdorf had intended to visit Switzerland for this purpose, but apparently could not fit a trip into his busy schedule.

Another composer whose music often reflects the glory of the Swiss Alps is Franz Liszt. Unlike Dittersdorf, Liszt traveled quite often to Switzerland in search of melody and inspiration. He seems to have found both on the Walensee, a rather forbidding body of water which no one else in his right mind would consider musically inspiring. But old Liszt was inspired enough, probably because of the countess who was rowing him around the lake. She was Marie d'Agoult, and she no doubt made up for any inspiring qualities lacking in the general landscape. In any case, Liszt wrote a piano piece on this lake, calling it *Au lac de Walenstadt*, and including it in his cycle, *Années de Pèlerinage* (Years of Pilgrimage). Interestingly enough, wherever he went with the countess, Liszt was singularly inspired. He saw countless things he might never have observed without her. And this is why he called her the "countless countess".

The first year of *Années de Pèlerinage* was reserved for Switzerland, and in the work Liszt included some typical Swiss motifs, as in the *Chapel of William Tell*, *Obermann Valley* and *The Bells of Geneva*. As far as can be determined, Liszt was also the only composer of note to be directly inspired by alpine flora. After picking numerous types of gentians and primulas during a visit to Switzerland in 1833, Liszt carefully pressed them in a book of music paper in order to preserve them for later inspiration and memories. When he opened the book some three years later, he noticed that the alpine flowers, with their strong colors, had left their imprint on the blank music paper. With extreme care, he circled the blue and red marks with his music pen. They had formed a perfect series of melodies – a unique case of direct inspiration from flower to paper!

Liszt was beside himself. He rushed down to the dock and called to the Countess d'Agoult, who was rowing her boat in the distance (the name of the lake is unfortunately obscure). Marie apparently thought that too much of this pilgrimage business was getting Franz down, for she rowed as fast as she could to find out what was wrong.

"Countess," Franz cried out as she approached the wharf, "the alpine flowers have for me a melody written!"

"Oh, Franzerl!" said Marie. "What will you name this piece?"

"There is but one name possible," replied Liszt. "I am compelled to call this composition *Fleurs mélodiques des Alpes*. Whatever I in the future will do, or wherever I shall be, I shall always remember the way the Swiss flowers have dirtied up my music paper!"

Richard Wagner also came to Switzerland for inspiration as well as to avoid all the people to whom he owed money. "If I am ever to repay my debts," he is once reputed to have said, "then I must go somewhere where the air is clear, where the pine scent and the sea gulls form a curious admixture for the prolongation of my unique art."

After visiting Switzerland, Wagner realized that

this was what he had been seeking. "Let me create more works like those which I conceived in that serene and glorious Switzerland, with my eyes on the beautiful gold-crowned mountains; they were masterpieces and nowhere else could I have conceived them." Here again, as in the case of Franz Liszt, Switzerland was doing its inspirational job. And here again, there was a woman to make the inspiration more believable.

Wagner's friend was Mathilde Wesendonk, and although she had no title – being the wife of a wealthy Zurich merchant – she owned several rowboats and quite a few houses to put them and anything else in. Mathilde put Wagner in one of her houses so that he could write bigger and longer operas – and the idea apparently paid off. Among other works, *Siegfried* – or at least parts of it – is the result of Wagner's love affair with Mathilde and Zurich. Mathilde was also a poetess, and Wagner, in order not to appear a complete ingrate, set some of her poems to music. They were *Der Engel* (The Angel), *Träume* (Dreams), *Schmerzen* (Pain), *Stehe still* (Stand Still) and *Im Treibhaus* (In the Doghouse). Wagner wrote another well-known song, *Waltzing Mathilde*, while in Zurich, and he dedicated it to the chargé d'affaires from Australia, who took a particular liking to his operatic efforts.

Although he never would have admitted it, Brahms would simply not have been Brahms without Switzerland. Here we think of the plaintive alphorn melody in the fourth movement of his First Symphony. In 1868, while visiting Switzerland, Brahms heard an alphorn blow this melody, and he immediately wrote down the notes for posterity and for Clara Schumann, to whom he sent them, along with an accompanying poem:

Hoch auf 'm Berg, tief im Tal
Grüss ich Dich vieltausendmal
(High on the mountains, deep in the valley,
I send you greetings many thousand times)

Brahms would not have liked the way this poem sounds in English, which is why he wrote it in German. But here again we must bow in reverence before the ageless inspiration of Switzerland, which provided the stuff of which great symphonies are made. Brahms had no Countess d'Agoult with him on the Swiss lakes (he preferred to row himself when he lived in Rüschlikon, on the Lake of Zurich). Nor was there a Mathilde Wesendonk with her villas and poems. Only Clara Schumann, sitting far away and believing in the greatness of Johannes Brahms.

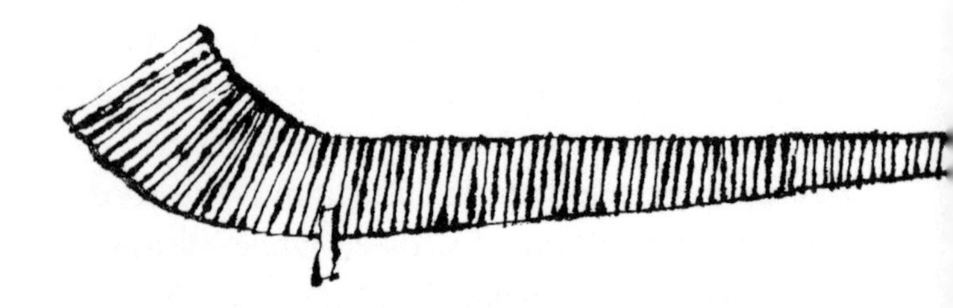

Stam̄
Tisch

Clubs and Trophies

I have just learned that there are more clubs, or *Vereins*, in Switzerland than there are people. This fact encouraged me to look into the matter further. Now, in the interests of international understanding and goodwill (and after months of careful study), I am prepared to make public the results of my analysis.

First of all, it is important to realize that without *Vereins* Swiss democracy simply would not work. The clubs offer an opportunity for the meeting of minds, a chance to air the pros and cons of the ever more complex issues which constantly face a working democracy.

What are these clubs and what is their significance? To understand this, one must project oneself into the life of the average Swiss male. Everyone enjoys camaraderie, and the Swiss is no exception. And because each Swiss male of voting age belongs, according to my analysis, to 5.27 clubs, he has free access to his fellow voters. Perhaps more important – and here the type of club plays a role – it gives him opportunity to engage in his favorite sports, like card-playing, beer-drinking and smoking.

Many citizens believe in a more active form of sport, like bird-watching, chess-playing or fishing – and almost every Swiss community of more than 100 inhabitants includes such pastimes in its official list of available *Vereins*. I made a particular study of the Bird-Watching and Bowling Clubs of Wahnsins, a village in the Knirps Valley, because, it seemed to me, the town offered conditions which could be classified as typical of all of Switzerland.

The Bird-Watching Club of Wahnsins was founded three years ago this month, and I was thus able to partake in the festivities on the occasion of its triennial anniversary. Like all clubs, it meets in a particular inn once each week. When I visited them, they were meeting in the Gasthof zum Schmerz, where all their trophies and club banners were displayed for the benefit of posterity. There were trophies for the most birds observed and trophies for unusual birds, trophies from other clubs and copies of trophies presented to other clubs during anniversary dinners, which take place twice each week.

This particular evening, the members of the Bowling Club (eight of whom were members of the Bird-Watching Club) were official guests of the Bird-Watching Club (eleven of whose members were in the Chess Club). Since fourteen of those present were also in six other clubs, it would have been inconsiderate and discourteous not to invite the members of those clubs as well. Thus half the population of Wahnsins (the men)

1.
Rang
1
2
4

were present as the mayor stood up to greet his fellow club citizens.
After a solemn introduction befitting the occasion, the mayor announced that a special trophy, commemorating the evening, was to be given to the Bowling Club. He asked the president of the club to step forward so that the ceremony could proceed. There was no response.
"Mr. Mayor," said Vogel J. Pflügel, president of the Bird-Watching Club, "you are the president of the Bowling Club – since last Saturday night, remember?"
"Oh yes, of course," countered the mayor, "how silly of me. But I cannot present this gorgeous silver plate to myself, it must come from someone else."
This posed a knotty procedural problem, such as many Swiss citizens face each day in their working democracy. After some moments of deliberation, the vice-chairman of the Fishing Club, Helmholtz Hecht, offered to conduct the ceremony as *ex officio* chairman. A vote was taken. (The members agreed – with three abstentions and five incorrectly marked ballots – to continue so that the evening could be concluded before *Polizeistunde*, the officially designated bedtime for the community.)
Helmholtz Hecht then took the floor. He pointed out that few organizations in Wahnsins had done

as much to support local industry as had the Bowling Club. The director of the largest local industry seconded the remark and personally thanked the club – and all the clubs in the Knirps Valley. "Without you," he said gratefully, "our brewery would not today be among the most important in Switzerland. You have all helped to support our international slogan:

"*When beer is near, there's cheer, my dear.*"

The club members then proposed a collective toast to themselves, followed by another. A general discussion then took place among working committee officers on new developments and progress made during the previous six days. The acting president of the Chess Club announced that a commission had been appointed to study the feasibility of increasing the squares on a chessboard by one.

"Point of order!" a voice called. "I agree with the hypothesis and the supposition," said the voice, "but my colleagues and I want to know whether you plan to increase the white squares or the black squares."

A vote was taken. It was agreed to send the matter back to committee to study the practicality of adding one red square with a white cross in it to the sixty-four existing squares of the common chessboard. This square would be a resting-place for weary traveling kings and queens, a spot to relax on when not facing the hectic battle of the outside world.

The assemblage cheered. The chairman of the Feathered Friend Committee of the Bird-Watching Club proposed a toast to the Chess Club and suggested that a special commemorative coin be struck, since this evening would go down in history. A vote was taken.

The proposal was accepted, with two articles added, the most important of which was that everyone present would receive a miniature copy – in bronze – of the actual coin, and that each club would receive an original copy for its trophy case.

There the matter rested while the club members exchanged pleasantries with each other and took time out to eat. Since this was a special occasion, the chef of the Gasthof zum Schmerz had prepared a special meal consisting of Sharkfin Soup, *Saumon fumé* and *Bratwurst avec roesti*, with assorted Swiss cheeses for dessert.

As the evening drew to a close, the mayor stood up again. "My trophy – I haven't received the trophy I was going to give myself!" Horrified expressions crossed the faces of everyone. "Where is my trophy? It's gone and lost forever!" the mayor cried.

From one of the back tables a shriek was heard.

"Was that silver plate the *bowling* trophy?" asked the shriek. "Heavens to William Tell, I just ate my *Bratwurst avec roesti* off of it!"
After a brief discussion, it was agreed to have the plate washed and polished and presented by the mayor to the president of the Bowling Club during the next meeting.
"But Mr. Mayor," said Vogel J. Pflügel, of the Bird-Watching Club, "you can't do that. You forgot again that *you* are the president of the Bowling Club!" The assemblage then took the information under advisement and a vote was taken.

Schlabouch

I've never met anyone in all my years in Switzerland who wasn't an expert on the country. This may seem to be an exaggerated statement, it may smack of yellow journalism, it may be irresponsible to the core. But it's true. Everybody *is* an expert here: I'm an expert – so are my wife and my children and our cleaning woman. That's one of the risks of living in Switzerland. Everybody expects us to know everything about the country – its history, its weather, its culture and philosophical thought, its train schedules, plane schedules, its voltage, boats and ski lifts. We must know its museums and cinemas and restaurants. Its culinary specialties we must not only have tried, but must also vouch for – on penalty of death or something worse.

We are also considered guilty of perjury should we fail to anticipate the exact cost and degree of enjoyment of a night on the town, including goulash soup at midnight. Actually, it may come as a surprise to visitors that most of us (I take the liberty of speaking for my fellow Americans) also work for a living. What we do varies, but what we have in common is that we are constantly boning up on facts and figures about Switzerland in anticipation of the avalanche of tourists who drop in on us both regularly and unexpectedly.

SCHLABOUCH

BAR

The technique of dropping-in generally follows a pattern, although I should point out that there are two distinct breeds of dropper-inners. The first is the friend of a friend who heard, mind you, that we were now living in Switzerland and isn't that just grand and what do we recommend for him to see. The other variety – and this form should not be taken lightly – is the visiting fireman, either an executive of the company we represent abroad or, sometimes worse, another company with which we do a reasonable amount of business. Whichever direction the visit takes, the questions asked are similar. We reconstruct here a typical battle of wits:

Question: "Was there really a Year of the Alps?"

Answer: "Why, yes indeed, there really was – and just a few years ago, too."

"I thought that the Alps were in Switzerland every year. I mean, was there a difference that year?"

"Well, you see, it was different because of the centennial of the establishment of St. Moritz and Davos and Schlabouch as world-famous alpine winter resorts."

"Oh! St. Moritz *is* in Switzerland! How nice, and I knew it all the time. And Davos I know and what did you say was the name of the other place?"

"Schlabouch. That's where we go every year,

sometimes twice a year. It's sort of – well, you could call it a Shangri-la, if you wanted to coin an expression. Schlabouch is a very special kind of resort."

"Please tell me about it, I'm all ears. I mean, it's *off* the beaten track, isn't it?"

"It's both off and on the beaten track, depending on what track you take. But the magnificent thing about Schlabouch is its setting – right on the most beautiful alpine terrace imaginable, where the people are quadrilingual and where the weather is always perfect. If it's raining in Zurich, the sun is shining in Schlabouch. And there's always snow in winter, and the food is magnificent – a combination of the best of the French, Italian, German and Liechtenstein cuisines – at prices almost anyone can afford. What's more, there's always room in Schlabouch, and there's no traffic to speak of and the air is clear and there's a lake for swimming and fishing in summer and for ice skating and curling in winter. And in the fall there are sailboats and in the spring it's a bird sanctuary. All in all, Schlabouch has everything."

"But does it have local color, too? And night life?"

"Sir, the expression *après-ski* was created in Schlabouch, where life after dark would startle Paris. And as for local color, Schlabouch reminds one of the quaintest Swiss music box – the chalets with their checked curtains dot the slopes surrounding the village and the cows wear genuine guaranteed Swiss cowbells. Schlabouch, in short, is perfection itself – for the tourist and for the indigenous population.

"And there are festivals, festivals galore, especially this year. Here again, Schlabouch is something out of the ordinary. In summer, there is the traditional Kirsch-drinking competition, featuring participants from eighteen countries, with a small plot of ground for the winner. And I'm sure you've heard of the famous Swiss bell-ringers and flag-wavers."

"It all sounds so *won*-der-ful!"

"Not only that, but as Switzerland's most famous poet, Gottfried von Unten, wrote almost a century ago, Schlabouch is 'ein wunderbarer Platz'. Furthermore, in the second stanza of *An Ode to My Swiss Abode*, he wrote that Schlabouch has absolutely no horseflies. In fact, the only thing wrong with the place is that nobody can pronounce it. But I always recommend it anyway, for Schlabouch has everything – even though it's fairly hard to find."

The Föhn

There are all kinds of winds in the world. Whirlwinds and tempests, hurricanes and typhoons, mistrals, siroccos and simooms. But there is no wind more insidious, more completely unpredictable, than the *Föhn* in Switzerland.

The odd thing about the Föhn is that few people know anything about it, except that it blows from the south, that it is a warm wind and that it encourages people to do strange things. And there is nothing stranger than doing strange things in Switzerland. Why a simple, old-fashioned sort of wind should have such great powers over a country as immovable as the Rock of Gibraltar is of some importance to the serious student of Switzerland.

I have personally spent more than a decade studying the odd meanderings of this wily wind. I have examined the Föhn as closely as anyone can investigate a wind. I have read of the Föhn in the works of authors who visited Switzerland and wrote of their experiences with the wind. I have collected horrible tales of devastation caused by the Föhn and stories of its hypnotic effect in countless legends and fables. Now, in the interests of greater scientific understanding, I am finally prepared to divulge the results of my research. The following information has been extracted from my study, which originally appeared under the title *The Föhn – A Mystery in Meteorological Metaphysics*.

What makes the Föhn so difficult for the average foreigner to understand is the fact that the word itself is so difficult to pronounce. If you say it correctly, it should come out sounding like the wind: a low, moaning groan beginning in the southern part of the esophagus and gushing forth out of the upper reaches of the lower palate. This is truly the Föhn. For people who don't know what an *Umlaut* is, the word can be written "*Foehn*", but the missing two dots make no difference to the pronunciation. The best way to pronounce it is with a slightly affected British accent and have it rhyme with "burn" or "turn". Drop the "r" and it should be quite easy.

Pronouncing "Föhn" is only the beginning, but nevertheless an important part of learning to live in Switzerland. The reason for this is that the Föhn is not only a wind, it is a magnificent excuse for not doing – or not being able to do – something.

For example, your mother-in-law who lives in Bisendingen near Winterthur wants to visit you on Thursday evening for just an hour or two. You quickly look out at the mountains – and herein lies an important aspect of the Föhn's powers. The mountains appear to be terribly close, and they seem to be moving closer and closer as one watches them.

"Aha!" says our anonymous friend with the mother-in-law. "The Föhn is blowing up a storm in the mountains and will no doubt continue to do so through Thursday. I shall tell mama-in-law that I can't see her because of the Föhn."

When I first heard stories of this kind, I thought the whole place was falling apart at the seams. What could a blasted wind have to do with one's parents-in-law? This was actually the beginning of my study of the Föhn.

The Föhn makes everyone a meteorologist. With the Föhn around there is no need for thermometers, barometers, hygrometers and anemometers. The good old bones of the human frame supply all the information that these instruments can, and in a much shorter span of time. For when the Föhn blows, everyone feels just lousy. It is said that no one *wants* to feel good when the Föhn blows. For without it, there is no justifiable reason for doing poor work, for not being able to think and for generally taking life a bit easier than when there is no Föhn.

When I first began studying the Föhn, I was convinced that it did not blow very often. I learned that the Föhn was not simply a southern wind, but one created by pressure differences on the northern and southern sides of the Alps. When

the pressure drops on the northern side – or perhaps it's the other side, I'm not quite sure – a vacuum or something similar is created. And then the Föhn, which has been lying around dormant somewhere above Lugano, enjoying the quiet life of Southern Switzerland, is bodily pulled up the face of the Alps. When our placid wind reaches the peak of the Gotthard Pass it smashes at high speed into, or out of, the vacuum I mentioned earlier. Unable to turn back on itself, it rolls into the valleys of Northern Switzerland, swooshing down the peaceful flanks of the Alps like a roller coaster in an amusement park. The Föhn draws with it the generally nicer weather of the south as well, causing thrillingly beautiful sunsets. But such sunsets often go unappreciated, for no one feels poetically inclined when he's got a headache.

The reason for the headaches is that people normally have headaches – not every day, of course, but every once in a while. The Swiss maintain that the Föhn makes aching bones feel achier, and I think we should let them continue to think so. If you laugh at the Föhn there is no doubt that you are a foreigner. It takes three years and five months, according to my survey, to become completely assimilated and to begin believing fervently in the powers of the Föhn. After two years or so, you give up fighting the Föhn protagonists, for there is little purpose in displaying one's ignorance in this country of weather experts.

When you first learn to speak German and someone asks you how you're feeling, you reply, "Gut, danke". Later, when you have been initiated to the cult of the Föhn and someone asks how you are, you do the following: you shift your weight uneasily from one foot to the other and you gaze through glazed eyes at the floor. Slowly raising your head, you reply, "Der Föhn". That's all there is to it. Learn to believe in the Föhn and your language improves instantly. Whatever is asked of you can be refused. As a matter of fact, I remember walking through an office recently in search of someone from whom I could ask some information. Every time I approached an employee, I got the same answer: "It's Föhn today."

Actually, I don't believe in the Föhn anymore. The scientific information I turned up in the course of my ten-year study has proved, once for all, that a simple wind could not possibly have so strong an effect on the human organism. It is also completely fallacious to believe that the Föhn blows as frequently as it is reputed to. People often claim to have Föhn headaches when the *Bise* – a cold northern wind – is blowing. Not I. I always have a *Bise* headache when the Föhn is blowing ... and my writing ... is always just as clear ... and concise ... as the Föhn the Föhn the Föhn – you beautiful gust of wind – will allow.

Good Wood

My friend Walti called me one evening, and instead of saying "good evening" he said "good wood". I knew that he had been working hard and that the strain was beginning to take its toll. Poor Walti, I thought. But I tried to humor him anyway.

"Good wood to you too," I said. "How are all the chips off the old block?"

"If you mean my children, they're fine. But apparently you don't understand the meaning of 'good wood' or you certainly would know what I'm getting at! The expression *gut Holz* – in German – is what one bowler says to another. It's the equivalent of wishing a skier friend a broken neck and leg when he goes on holiday."

"Oh," I said, "I thought 'good wood' might be a reference to the quality of our furniture, which, as you know, is made of the finest aged poplar. And I like our furniture – I really do – even *with* the oranges in it."

"Stop digressing," Walti replied. "I'm calling for a reason. Our bowling club is short one member since our ace broke his leg skiing last week. Would you like to bowl with us tonight?"

I regretted everything I had thought about Walti's having overworked. I replied that I would be delighted to bowl with the club, even though I

had never bowled in Switzerland. "Thanks a lot, fellow bowler," I said. "See you in ten minutes... and good wood!"
Bowling alleys in Switzerland are almost always located in a local inn or restaurant – usually in the cellar. There is a reason for this, one having to do with the fact that the alleys are then relatively close to where the wine and beer are stored.
When I met Walti and the other eight members of his bowling club, I was promptly introduced to the traditions and lore of the sport. We all spent ten minutes shaking hands and wishing each other good wood. This made forty-five handshakes, although my arithmetic could be wrong. In any case, the evening now began in earnest. Walti picked up a telephone which was on the table and mumbled something into the receiver. I was sure these were some sort of cryptic orders to the pinboy – if this was indeed what they called the person who sets up the bowling pins.
"What did you say on the telephone?" I asked him when he hung up. "What I said? Nothing special. I just ordered three bottles of wine and six beers, that's all."
"Excuse me for asking," I asked, "but when do we start bowling? I'm most eager to learn what I can."
"Oh yes, of course," said Walti. "As soon as the

drinks arrive and after the traditional bowling toasts."
"The bowling toasts... what's that mean?"
Walti did not have a chance to reply, for just then the waitress entered. When the wine and beer had been served, Walti stood up. He proceeded to say a few words relating to how nice it was that we could all be together on such a lovely evening in such a pleasant place under such fine conditions. He welcomed me, as a representative of a foreign country – a person, he said, whose interest in Switzerland was deep and genuine, as would be proved by the evening still ahead of us.
"Gut Holz!" Walti said as he held up his glass in a gesture of good fellowship.
"Gut Holz!" the general membership repeated.
"Who has a one-franc piece?" asked one of my new friends. I produced the coin. It was handed from one member to the other along the long bench in front of the bowling alley proper. Then Walti dropped it into a slot in the bowling alley control center, and the pins appeared automatically at the end of the alley.
A young woman was elected to begin the session. She stood up, chose a ball and began to swing it back and forth. I was amazed at her strength, for these balls are not especially light. She let go of the ball, and a moment later the pins seemed to explode.

"Bravo!" I screamed. "A strike, a complete and utter strike – the best possible score!"
"Control yourself," said Walti. "That was good, to be sure, but it was only a *Säuli* or 'piglet'." I had noticed the sign light up with a pig on it, but I had not realized what it meant. "The best in Swiss bowling," continued Walti, "is a *Kranz* or 'wreath', where the middle pin is left standing. This is considered far more difficult and is therefore accorded a higher score than a piglet. Now it's your turn," said Walti. I looked behind me. "*Your* turn," he said again.
If a wreath was the best possible score, I must shoot for one, I thought. I chose a big brown ball with two holes in it – one for the thumb, one for assorted other fingers. I took a professional-looking stance at the head of the alley and glared mercilessly at the pins at the other end. I swung the ball back... once, twice, three times... and released it. I am not sure whether it was a good shot or not. It did describe a beautifully full and even arc before it bounced out of our alley and into the neighboring one. Once there, it hit the side of the alley and bounded back to the middle, knocking over all the pins.
"Triple darn!" I mumbled. "And I wanted to leave one pin standing!" There were faint shouts coming from the alley where I had made my *Säuli*. I heard everybody saying that word over

9
egle sanft und nicht als Flegel!
Sonst verdirbst Du Bahn und
Kegel!
der WIRT

and over again, and I felt proud. Walti told me that they were swearing at me, but how could I believe him?

"Now," said Walti, "sit down and have a glass of wine, and I'll try to explain something about the game. There's an old expression – you can see it over there on the wall. In German it says:

Kegle sanft und nicht als Flegel
Sonst verdirbst du Bahn und Kegel.

This means that you must not throw the ball – just aim and gently roll it towards the pins. If you set the ball down in front of the line, everyone has the right to call you a *Sandhase*, which means 'sand bunny'."

I had no idea where such an expression could have originated, since Easter was long past. But I was enjoying this lesson in bowling – and it was so relaxing, especially with the fine Swiss wine I was drinking.

"When do I shoot again?" I asked.

"In a minute," Walti replied. "As soon as everyone has bowled once."

"In that case, I'll step outside for some fresh air. I'll be right back."

It was a clear Swiss night. The lights on the mountains twinkled from across the lake, and the moon – now almost full – was reflected in the water. It was so peaceful. Just the rumble of bowling balls in the distance and the crack of pins as they reached their target. How magnificent, I thought. All this natural beauty – the moon, the lake, the mountains and the traditional sport of bowling. What a combination!

I re-entered the alley and sat down. Walti said that I had missed my turn and would have to wait for the next round. This time I decided to stay and watch the progress of the game. I soon noticed that Walti's club seemed to be doing quite well. The women were, for the most part, even better than the men – at least I thought so. I mentioned this to Walti and he said that I was most observant. I was flattered.

It was my turn now. This time I was determined to bowl carefully, to show everyone that I wasn't so bad after all. Ready, aim ... fire! Now the ball seemed radar-controlled. It left my hand delicately and deftly. It appeared to gather momentum as it headed for the center pin... and through the middle! I was too excited to look! Then I opened my eyes and observed that my shot had indeed gone through the middle – and knocked over exactly three pins. How bitter my shame!

"Congratulations!" my bowling friends said in chorus. "Ninety points for the *Gasse*." Walti came up to me and placed his arm around my shoulder. "That was a beautiful *Gasse* or 'alley'. Right down the middle!"

I was confused. Now how was that again? When all the pins are knocked over, this is good – but not quite as good as when one is left standing. Next on the list was my *Gasse*, where only three pins were knocked over. I hesitated to ask what the absolute best was for fear that someone would tell me to leave all the pins standing for a total of ten thousand points.

But why fight tradition? This had been a most enjoyable evening of wine and bowling, and I shall probably go down in local history as the first foreign visitor to achieve so remarkable a score – and on two different alleys.

"Good night," I said to everyone as the evening drew to a close. "Good *wood*," said Walti. "Now you're one of us!"

Switzerland and the News

Switzerland is not a country of momentous events. It has a fairly stable form of government, and demagogues find little following – and a great deal of resistance – in any part of the country. Hence political coups, military juntas, torchlight parades and all the other items which make front-page news everywhere else are noticeably absent in Switzerland.

Even crime, which appears to be gaining in popularity throughout the world, has a hard time gaining acceptance among the Swiss, for not only do they dislike violence in any form, but they also resist change – and crime represents change, among other things. With both crime and political excess so unpopular, what, then, remains for the country's newspapers to report?

There is, of course, enough happening outside Switzerland to slake the thirst of any good Swiss citizen in search of vicarious experience in his daily newspaper. Wars and assassinations, riots and revolutions: everywhere, but not in Switzerland. Some people consider it almost shameful, but Switzerland has not experienced a major labor dispute or strike for as long as anyone can remember.

Now, on to the news of the month as it might be reported – in German, French or Italian – in a local newspaper. Incidentally, Switzerland enjoys the highest per capita newspaper readership, and the largest number of newspapers per capita, in the world – or so one is told. Latest figures show that there are 1.37 daily or weekly newspapers per healthy Swiss citizen, not including women or foreign workers. Though the economics of supporting so many journals would seem problematical to the outside observer, it is worth noting here that every Swiss – including the women – reads an average of 14 papers each day, only some of which he actually subscribes to or buys, but the majority of which he peruses over coffee and *pâtisserie* in his neighborhood tea-room. Now, on – once more – to the news of the month!

World Football Champions Will Holiday in Appenzell

Appenzell (U & I) – Enthusiasm for the World Championship football match in England extended even to Appenzellerland, the two demi-cantons of Appenzell Inner-Rhoden and Appenzell Outer-Rhoden in Northeastern Switzerland. Using the Northeast Swiss Tourist Association and the Swiss Football Federation as go-betweens, the enterprising owner of the largest hotel in the town of Appenzell has invited the entire British team, the new World Champions, to spend a winter holiday in the attractive village at the foot of the

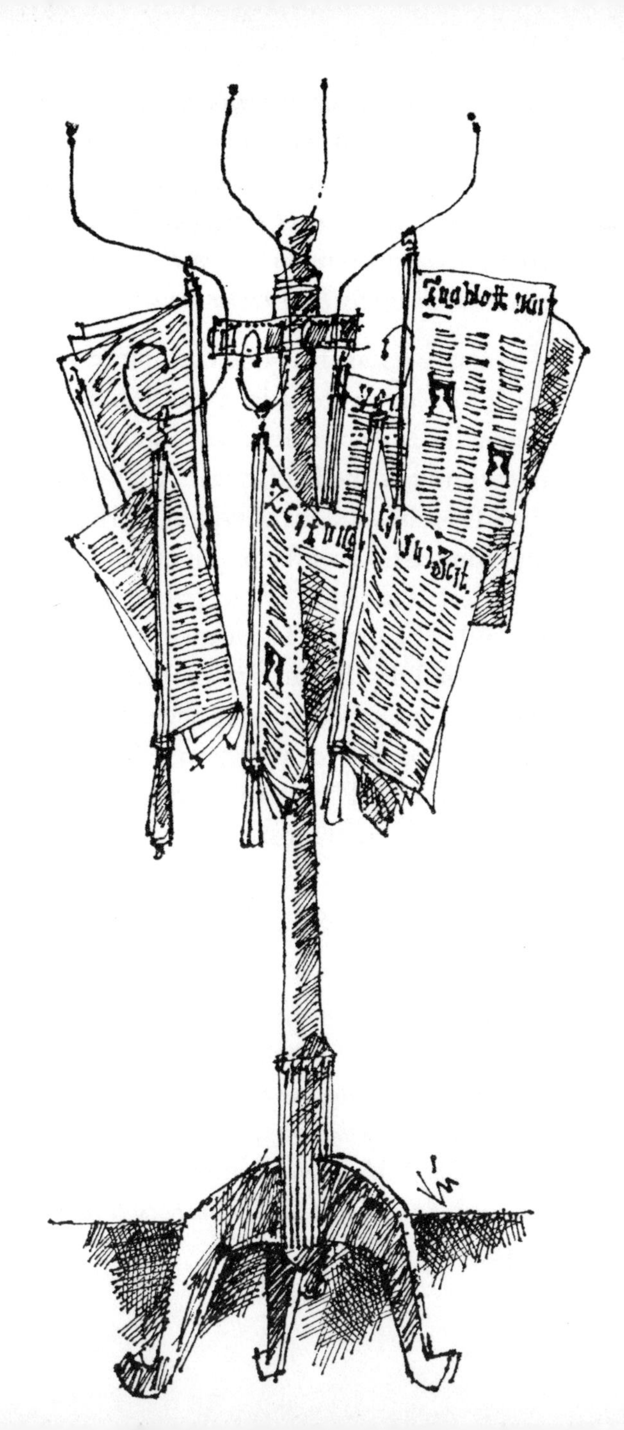
Zeitung
Zeit.

Säntis. The reply was surprisingly fast in coming – and it was positive. But the Secretary of the British Football Association asked that the generous host be patient until June or July of next year, since the team, hurrying from one match to another, has no chance to think about vacations during the busy winter season.

The above release is a good example of what must go into a news story in Switzerland. Note the humanitarian approach: an enterprising hotel owner invites the British team for a winter holiday. This shows signs of typical Swiss generosity and compassion for the plight or our fellow men, or at least the plight of our fellow football players. What happens? The team, too busy to take a winter holiday in January or February, accepts the kind invitation to take their winter holiday "in June or July of next year". This sounds as though it could be a slap at Britain's fabled summer climate, but it must have been unintentional.

Newly Announced Numismatic Society Names Newcomers

Geneva (A & P) – The International Numismatic Society, meeting at nearby Cointrin, announced today that it was according full membership to delegates of all countries where coins are accepted as official currency. Remington J. Mint, president of the society, referred the question of what constitutes a coin back to committee for decision during the society's next meeting. Delegates of the West Archipelagian Republic walked out of the meeting when it was decided that small discs cut out of old oil drums were not acceptable under the generic definition of a coin, i.e., "a piece of metal stamped and issued by the authority of the government for use as money." Mr. Mint regretted the decision taken by the West Archipelagese and promised to place the weight of his office behind an early and equitable solution of the question. The delegate of Southern Liboomia suggested that a coin be flipped to decide the matter. Standing before the committee, he stated unequivocally, "Heads I win, tails you lose," in support of the motion, but his proposal was rejected. The flipping of coins, said Mr. Mint, was beneath the dignity – to coin a phrase – of so august a body, and could not be considered a reasonable, civilized method of arriving at important decisions in the modern world.

Here we have an excellent example of Switzerland as a focal point for international cooperation and discussion. There are so many meetings and conventions taking place each year in Switzerland that a special newspaper, the Zurich *Tagungsblatt*, was established to maintain a record of what is happening all over the country. The following story is typical of another of Switzerland's major interests: health and the Swiss climate.

New Zest for the Nervous System:
International Conference on the Medicinal Effects of the Alpine Climate Meets in Lugano

Lugano (B & B) – The empirical views which were held as early as 1860 on the influence of high-altitude climate on the human body have subsequently been confirmed by experimental research, with particular emphasis on the salutary effect which such climate has for sufferers from bronchial asthma. During the last century, the practical and empirical realization became widespread that people from the lowlands undergo certain fundamental changes during a lengthy stay in the Swiss Alps. In 1862, J. A. Weber wrote: "When a wanderer climbs in the Alps, or reaches their heights on horseback or by any other means of conveyance, to what a remarkable transformation is he subjected! If he suffered from loss of appetite, poor digestion, lack of blood, difficulty in breathing, inadequate muscular power, slackened nerves, dulled senses, a fettered spirit – his appetite awakens mightily, his digestion begins to function properly, breathing becomes easier and the skin gains a ruddy glow, his movements become more energetic, there is new zest for the nervous system, his humor lightens, his spirit awakens, is rejuvenated, refreshed, and his thoughts flow in easy movement."

And so we have the average Swiss, worrying about his neighbor's inadequate muscular power, his loss of appetite, his slackened nerves.

While he is concerned about these deficiencies – and it is not much different now from what it was in 1862, when Mr. Weber wrote on the subject – thousands of people are losing their lives in traffic accidents, uprisings, typhoons, floods, war and other forms of general violence. But in Switzerland the mountain air awakens one's appetite, and the "digestion begins to function properly".

My Telephone

It is generally conceded that the Swiss possess a unique gift for understanding the intricacies of technical things. That is why so many countries are envious of Switzerland – primarily because of the Swiss ability to put together a watch that works for a reasonable length of time. The watchmaker's skill seems to be symbolic of everything that borders on technical prowess, for Switzerland looks like a watch, ticks like a watch and thinks like a watch. The trouble is that some things do not resemble watches at all. Take the story of my telephone.

When I moved to Switzerland a number of years ago, I happened to live on the border between two communities, Herrliberg and Feldmeilen. Actually, for postal and taxation reasons, Feldmeilen decided to adopt me, with the result that Herrliberg was left out in the cold. However, Herrliberg – obviously jealous of Feldmeilen's acquisition of my family and apparently lacking a full quota of genuine artists on its home territory – decided to grant me a Herrliberg telephone number. This seemed fine for the moment, but it was also the beginning of the story of my telephone.

A friend once tried to obtain my telephone number through information and was told that I was nonexistent. "Nonexistent he isn't," said our acquaintance, "because he very much exists in Feldmeilen!"

"Impossible!" reiterated the telephone company. Our friend never did reach us that year and, as a result, I missed receiving a contract to write a Hollywood scenario based on Dante's *Inferno*. This film was eventually produced under the title "The Fires Are Burning for Me and My Gal".

Perhaps I had lost a hundred thousand dollars because I lived in Feldmeilen instead of Herrliberg, but, after all – and thanks to the telephone company – no one bothered me, for no one knew I existed.

One day, worried over the fact that our telephone had not rung once in two years, I called information to ask if they knew me.

"Sorry, sir," Miss Information said, "Eugene V. Epstein could not possibly live in Feldmeilen, for we have a Herrliberg number listed for him."

"My dear," I said, "please be kind enough to correct your records. I am Mr. Epstein himself and I live in Feldmeilen. But through the kindness and generosity of the telephone officials I was granted a Herrliberg number so that no one would telephone and distract me from my work, which, as you must certainly know, belongs to the ages – the ages of three to four."

"Sorry, Herr Eppschtein," said my new friend. "You couldn't possibly live in Feldmeilen. Why don't you take up the question with the Cantonal Address Office – they will advise you where you live even if you don't know it yourself."
"Miss," I implored, "just because I have a number beginning with the digits '90' doesn't mean I can't live in Feldmeilen!"
"Terribly sorry, sir, Feldmeilen begins with '73'. Adieu!"
Here I was, a man without a country, a man without a community. There was my telephone – that ominous instrument – looking as if it would ring any moment but obviously thinking better of it. If only someone would call me, I thought. If only someone would interrupt this incessant and boring writing. Ring, damn it!
"R-r-r-ring, rr-r-r-ing," went the telephone. I jumped across the room, tripping over the cat and my son's model watch factory, which ticks like a real one. "Hello!" I gasped into the receiver. "This is the telephone office, sir. We wish to inform you that your telephone number is going to be changed to one beginning with '73'. We are sorry to do this, but, for organizational reasons, all people, including women, who are now living in Feldmeilen will be given Feldmeilen numbers. Your new area telephone office will now be Rapperswil instead of Zurich."

The next day, while shopping for a new cat in Zurich, I called my wife. The number rang and rang – but there was no answer. Wait, I thought to myself, I must dial the new number. When I did, my wife answered immediately. The next minute I was on the wire with the telephone company.
"Madam," I uttered, "why does the old number seem to ring when it really doesn't? My wife answered only when I dialed the new number."
"Obviously!" said the telephone company. "What do you expect when you dial the wrong number?"
"That's fine," I interjected. "But what happens if a complete stranger should try to reach us under the old number and thinks it's ringing when it really isn't?"
"If it isn't, then you have nothing to worry about – he won't reach you anyway."
"Precisely!" I said, rapidly losing my famous composure. "But supposing he *wants* to reach me?"
"Then he should call the new number."
"Exactly! Supposing he doesn't know the new number?" I had her there.
"You must give the new number to all your friends," she said.
"But is it not possible for the telephone company to provide the new number when the old one is dialed?" She told me it was, but, after all, I was the one who had moved.

"Moved? Where did I move to?"
"You moved from Herrliberg to Feldmeilen – you should know that!"
"No, I didn't move, I swear it. The telephone company simply changed my number. It was as simple as that."
"Impossible, you must have moved. Why don't you check with the Cantonal Address Office and ask them your name and where you live?"
"Madam, I have been through this before. I happen to have lived in Feldmeilen for seven years, during which time I had the pleasure of a telephone number beginning with the indigenous digits '9' and '0'. It is only at this point that the telephone company apparently thought better of their past actions and decided – no doubt after a vote of all males present and forming a quorum – to change my number to one beginning with '73'."
"Oh then, sir, you must in any case speak with the Rapperswil area office. This is Zurich, and we have nothing to do with Feldmeilen numbers."
I dialed Rapperswil with a vengeance. "This is Eugene V. Epstein, and I'm calling about my former number which began with '90'."
"You must call Zurich, sir, we don't handle Herrliberg here."
"No, you don't understand! That was my *former* number. My present number begins with '73'."

"When did you move, sir?"
"Oh, darn it!" I said quietly, attempting to control my blood pressure. "I just wanted to ask you if you could conceivably tell anyone trying to call my old number that that number has been replaced by a newer number more indicative of the location in which I reside?"
"Why didn't you say so in the first place? These people who don't know how to express themselves! What you ask for, sir, is an exceedingly simple matter, only you will have to call Zurich, for they are in charge of your former number, which is, after all, the one your friends will dial."
I was exhausted, but managed, somehow, to thank the friendly lady from Rapperswil. I was now so intent on solving this problem that I sprained the tip of my index finger when I next dialed Zurich.
"Zurich? This is Eugene V. Epstein, telephone number 73..." She wouldn't let me say the rest of it, but informed me that such numbers are handled by Rapperswil.
I explained the story again, and the Zurich operator apparently understood me.
"We'll simply notify callers that your number has been changed," she said. "Then we'll tell them what the new number is."
"That would be dandy of you," I said graciously.
We then made all final arrangements and I hung

up, my faith in Swiss technological progress completely restored.

The next day, I thought I would double-check. I dialed the old number. It rang … and rang … and rang. Then a tape-recorded voice said, "The number you are calling is no longer valid. Please call number such-and-such for further information."

I whipped through the dial with my newly acquired dialing proficiency. "What number are you calling?" asked another voice. I told her.

"One moment, please."

I waited. Then the voice said that the number I was calling had been disconnected.

"Ha!" I shouted. "Now I have you! I am the subscriber himself, and that number has *not* been disconnected. It has been changed!" In the end, as one might suspect, the matter was straightened out, as things often are in Switzerland. I now know, for example, that my name is Eugene V. Rapperswil, that I live in Herrlistein near Winterthur, and that I have moved once every three years during my two-year stay in the country.

This really isn't fair to the telephone company, if you think of everything they have to do and the shortage of trained personnel these days. I am extremely patient and I realize that we live in a complicated and difficult age. It's just that I feel like moving to Herrliberg to see what they would do next time.

Glaciers Are Always Made of Ice

The question of how the earth is shaped has fascinated man for thousands of years. Actually, no one ever believed it was flat, except for various kings and queens – the ones, after all, who financed the early excursions of such men as Cristoforo Colombo, Marco Polo and Vincenzo Bellini. These valiant explorers certainly believed that the world was round, but they were afraid to say so for fear that the reigning monarchs would consider them out of their minds and cut them off without a single lira or peseta.

Edmondo P. Mondo was one of the first students of the shape of the earth, a science which at that time was called "Mondologia" or, in English, "Earthology". This was, of course, before Galileo Galilei returned from his scientific expedition to the Middle East, where he was studying the saline content of an inland sea subsequently named after him. It was Galileo who first used the term "geodesy" when he wrote his preliminary study, *La geodesia facile*, or "Geodesy Made Easy".

Here again we must thank Galileo for his efforts to lead us out of the dark ages into the age of enlightenment. One day, while trying to invent the telescope, Galileo looked out of his kitchen window, which faced north, and saw what seemed to be a slight curvature in the horizon. He immediately realized that he was witnessing a strange magnetic phenomenon, one that could, if properly documented, prove that the earth was round. But Galileo had had enough of this proving business. Every time he invented something – no matter what it was – he ran breathlessly to the authorities to describe to them the importance of his invention. It was all a waste of time, for, without fail, they took his invention away from him and told him to go home.

This is why it took twenty-five years longer to get the telescope invented – and the reason why at least thirteen telescopes were confiscated before Galileo found an official who was sympathetic and understanding. In the beginning, Galileo called his invention the "black cylinder". Only later, during a hitherto unchronicled visit to Switzerland, did he think of a better name.

Somewhere around the Lake of Lucerne, Galileo met up with Switzerland's national hero, William Tell, who was trying to figure out a way to save the country without killing his son. Galileo suggested the "black cylinder", which was still unpatented since no one in Italy believed that such an invention could really work. Tell took one look at it, and another look through it, and immediately sensed the importance of his new friend's invention.

"Listen, Galli," said Tell, "why don't you let me use this thing tomorrow when I shoot at that apple on my son's head? With this cylinder I'm sure to knock off the fruit without injuring my poor little boy."
"Excellent idea, old man," replied Galileo. "Go to it!"
And so it came to pass that William Tell, with the help of Galileo's "black cylinder", shot the apple off his son's head and rescued Switzerland. This is, of course, a well-known story. Generally unknown, however, is the fact that Galileo, overjoyed at the success of his invention, decided to name it after Switzerland's national hero. That is why, for so many years, Galileo's black cylinder was known as the "Williamscope".
Galileo was also interested in the earth's interior, and, while in Switzerland, decided to study the Alps. In a letter to his brother Gordon dated May 16, 1624, Galileo tells of his first experiences with the Alps:
"... When one thinks of how many strata of rock are necessary to create even one little Alp, then one can only stand in wonder before these creatures of Nature. It is my plan to study each of them, to examine every peak and every crevasse with my Williamscope and to note down for future generations some of my findings."
We know that Galileo prepared an exhaustive

study of the Swiss Alps and that these papers would undoubtedly have advanced the sciences of glaciology and volcanology by hundreds of years. Unfortunately, almost the entire collection was lost when a fierce southern wind known as the *Föhn* swept down from the mountains and blew Galileo's study all over Switzerland and even as far as the Black Forest. Galileo picked up as many papers as he could, but the rest were lost forever.

Today, it is interesting to roam the countryside looking for items of particular scientific value, in the footsteps, as it were, of the indomitable Galileo. Take the Aletsch Glacier, for example. Galileo describes it in one of the papers not blown away by the Föhn:

"There are glaciers and glaciers. But wherever there are glaciers, there is none more imposing than the Aletsch. I have walked all over it – up and down it, across and back and around again. My first and most important discovery was that my feet got cold. This may seem somewhat prosaic, but what earthly good is a scientist whose feet get cold every time he walks around a glacier? So I proceeded to line my shoes with some of the other scientific papers I had rescued from that brutal wind. The next time I walked on the Aletsch, everything was fine. I believe that I have also invented the principle of convectional insulation, for my feet are now pleasantly warm, my toes as snug as ten bugs in a rug.

"The glacier itself consists mainly of ice, with several layers of snow on top. The latter can be accounted for by the severe and snowy winters of the Valais region. In any case, one layer of snow has not had a healthy chance to melt before another begins to build up.

"I started to dig through the layers of snow in order to examine the consistency of the ice as well as its crystalline structure. The first day – after fixing my shoes – I dug through forty-three layers. Layer twenty-two was the thickest – ninety-one centimeters thicker than layer number four, which was the thinnest. Most of the layers were of finely packed powder snow, the best kind for skiing and other winter sports. Unfortunately, even though I have been working on the problem, skiing is still competely unknown here, and most people, except for children, hate the snow and winter generally.

"After I had diligently dug through the forty-third snow layer, I came upon the ageless ice of the Aletsch. How perfect it was – hard and blue and cold, as ice should be. I chipped out a piece to study more carefully. I blew at it and the moisture in my breath froze at once. I licked at it and my tongue stuck to it. It was indeed a *very* cold piece of ice!

"That day I continued to chip away at the glacier. After a few more centimeters, though, I grew tired of this experiment and returned to camp for some sustenance. My study of the Aletsch may not be the most detailed in all of glaciology, but I hope it provides some information of use to scientists of the future."

Many years were to pass before the lessons learnt from Galileo's glacial experiments could be utilized. For example, Galileo first verified the connection between low temperature and the formation of ice. The thermometer he carried happened to register −10° centigrade (14° Fahrenheit) and he noticed that water was always frozen at this temperature. Through a number of further tests Galileo was able, with a candle, to warm up the pieces of ice he took from the Aletsch and then let them freeze again, measuring each time the exact temperature as they froze.

He continued this series of experiments for four or five months. At the end of that time, he averaged the temperatures and concluded that the ice of the Aletsch Glacier began to turn to water at 1° centigrade (33° Fahrenheit). Conversely, water began to show signs of becoming ice at a temperature of approximately 0° centigrade (32° Fahrenheit). Galileo's discoveries, although primitive by today's standards, have been extremely helpful to countless numbers of glaciologists the world over.

Galileo also recognized the relationship between altitude, atmospheric pressure and temperature. He knew that it became colder the higher one climbed, even if it was warm when one started. He knew, too, that the air became thinner and that pressure diminished. He devised the first successful formula for boiling eggs at high altitudes, one still used by many mountain hotels in Switzerland.

"The degree of albuminous viscosity of a boiling chicken egg," wrote Galileo, "is in large part determined by the height of the vessel in which it is being prepared. If the vessel is at sea level, the egg may be cooked to a pleasant degree of doneness in three to four minutes. However, for every hundred meters of altitude added, one must allow a further nine seconds of boiling to achieve the same result."

This document, "Ten Tasty Ways to Boil Eggs in a Mountainous Country", could not have been written had Galileo never visited Switzerland. Only here was he able to transport his boiling egg – step by step – from the depths of the valleys to the heights of the highest Alps. As a result, Galileo deduced that it takes the longest time to cook an egg when one is trying to do it on the highest mountain, like the Jungfrau or the Matterhorn. In addition, the constant winds keep blowing out the cooking flame, so that it often requires an hour or more to finish the job. This can, of course, lead to further complications if there are a lot of hungry people waiting for breakfast in the Alps.

The Creative Urge

Everyone who visits Switzerland has the desire to express himself in writing, for the creative urge is strong in the Alps. According to a recent survey, however, only one traveler out of twenty-seven thousand actually places pen to paper with the intention of describing what he has seen and felt in Switzerland. The others *want* to write, though, and it is only a question of helping them shed their frustrations and complexes, and teaching them that almost everyone can become a world-famous writer.

Over the years, Switzerland has been chosen as the scene of many literary works – from Sherlock Holmes to the modern spy thriller. The country seems to cast a strange, magnetic spell over visiting authors. Its role is generally a passive or scenic one, for, as everybody knows, nothing quite compares to Swiss scenery.

The Swiss are interested in encouraging the mention of their country in international literature. That is why a new organization has been founded to further latent literary talents among tourists. This group, called the Swiss Writers Inspiration Guild (SWIG), is dedicated to the basic philosophy that "If you cannot describe it to your wife or husband, however can you write about it?" SWIG has an enormous job to do, and the organization's efforts are worthy of the highest recognition. Its first project, known as "Operation Big Alp", involved handing out two million leaflets with the rules of SWIG's first international contest, which promised free holidays to those visitors who could best describe a Swiss mountain, either in prose or poetry.

The President of SWIG, Louis M. Quinze, announced recently that he was extremely heartened by the results of this first contest. Many people who never wrote before have now done so, and, according to Mr. Quinze, the country is "literally crawling with authors".

"Some camera manufacturers have complained that tourists are taking fewer photographs," Mr. Quinze added, "but, by the same token, sales of ballpoint pens and paper have more than trebled in recent months." He also mentioned that "tourists are examining everything more carefully than they did in the past. Whenever they see a lake, for instance, they try to establish its color – blue, green or brown – then its size, then the surrounding area."

We are pleased to present here some of the first efforts of tourists to describe the natural wonders of Switzerland. Mrs. Arthur Choke, a visitor from Baker, Alaska, submitted the following description on her contest form:

Look up at the mountains! Are they not something
Upon which to look at up to? Why did I
Not come sooner so that I could look up
At them from down here earlier?

There is inspiration in these lines. The steering committee of the Geneva Automobile Society (GAS) considers Mrs. Choke's simple description to be among the most poignant it has ever received.

Another entry in the SWIG holiday contest was this delightful poem by a New York housewife. It was written on a postcard to her sister-in-law in the Bronx:

Youse guys who never seen this land
Are missin' out on somethin' grand!
There's nothin' here like old Broadway,
No Gimbel's, Macy's, ladies' day.
But they got lots of lakes and mountains,
Plenty of ice and drinking fountains,
Pretty girls and cheese and watches,
And herring which the Swiss call matjes.
All in all, it's lots of fun here.
I'll tell you more when I am back, dear.

One of the most remarkable efforts to be submitted to the SWIG contest judging committee was a short story by a young man from Threadington Briar, Coates-on-Hookes, England. For reasons of space, we can reproduce only the be-

ginning of this story, but readers will immediately notice that herein lies a budding talent:
"The night was dark and murky. Wisps of fog stood guard over the river, and the lights of the quay formed strange reflected patterns in the quiet water. An occasional gull fluttered its wings and broke the quiet with its nasal call. All was still, for it was midnight in Zurich.
"James Blond stood on the Vegetable Bridge gazing at the undulating ribbons formed by the lights on the River Limmat. He was thinking. The smoke from his gold-tipped cigarette curled serenely up over his powerful forehead and into the endless night, where it disappeared in the blackness. He was waiting.
"James Blond, secret agent zero-naught-cipher, suave, Continental, wily, shrewd – and dangerous! His knowledge of Europe's highways and byways, cobblestone lanes and back alleys had been put to good use by his government. It was in Switzerland, at the Reichenbach Falls, that Blond had single-handedly uncovered the super-secret Russian counterespionage agency SCHNOOCK and its master spy, Kropotkin, known as Krop the Pot. But that was years ago...
"Now it was thirty-five minutes past midnight on the Vegetable Bridge. James Blond flicked his cigarette into the Limmat and exhaled his last draught of tar-filled smoke. He was waiting.

"Special agent MNX, Blond's boss in London, had told him of the importance of this mission. If the Russians were to discover the secret formula of a newly developed Swiss fondue, they would steal it, and everybody in the world might then be crying for holey cheeses. James Blond knew what this meant. He had faced up to difficult situations before.

"The bells of the Fraumünster tolled one o'clock. Quiet now, thought Blond, he should be along any minute ... any minute. To his left, across the river and through the trees, Blond caught a glimpse of Kropotkin's chartreuse Oldsmobile turning regally into the Limmatquai. Blond jumped into his Ashton-Marlin, which was parked nearby, turned on the radarscope and headed out across Switzerland – towards Lucerne and Interlaken – in his continuing pursuit of Krop the Pot."

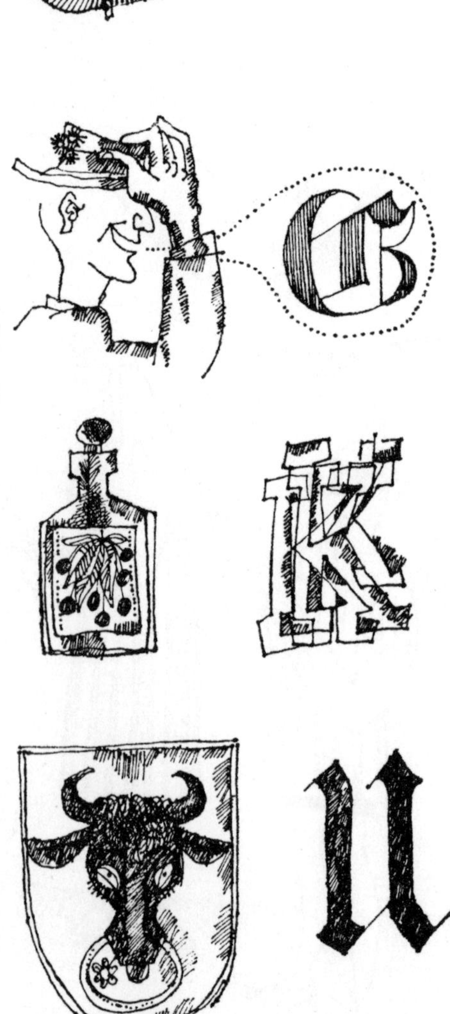

An Alpine Alphabet

A is for Alphorn, more than ten feet in length.
Those who can blow it are known for their strength.

B is for Building, a Swiss type of game,
Which goes on forever – and still looks the same.

C is for Cheese, the world's best if you please:
Tastes awfully good after carrots and peas.

D is for Dirt, which the Swiss always hate,
That's why they are cleaning from early to late.

E is for Eating, which all Swiss adore,
Begin with five portions, and then we'll have more.

F is for Fondue, a cheese kind of dish,
Some people dip and others just swish.

G is for *Grüezi*, the most used of words,
When you meet people, horses or birds.

H is for Happy, the happy Swiss people,
Who work like the devil and never sleeple.

I means Inspired, mostly from mountains,
But also from lakes and from very old fountains.

J is for *Jass*, a card game of skill,
Which every Swiss plays – the thought makes me ill.

K is for *Kirsch*, which some drink like wine,
There's quite a resemblance to fine turpentine.

L is for Lake, as in Lake of Lucerne,
But far more important is how much you earn.

M is for Money, taken with thanks,
Most kinds will do, especially francs.

N is for Nature, as most people know,
Now back to Nature with Jean Jacques Rousseau.

O means Official in countries like this,
Where following orders proves you are Swiss.

P stands for *Polizeistund'*, when everything closes,
When the Swiss go to sleep on their own beds of roses.

Q is for Quality, synonymous with "Swiss",
What milk, O what honey, what life and what bliss!

R is for *Rösti*, potatoes gone Swiss,
They're easy to make – it's just hit or miss.

S stands for Sausage, all succulent sorts.
What would life be without sausage and sports?

T is for Tourists, O welcome to all,
Come spend your money, then leave – we're so small.

U is for Uri, which rhymes with Missouri,
And is also a state which has trial by jury.

V means *Verboten*, or so we are taught,
Don't *do* it, don't *touch* it, or you will get caught!

W is for Watches and Winter and Wine,
Which, in itself, makes a perfect first line.

X marks the spot where the Swiss people swore
To settle their problems in peace, not in war.

Y is for Yodel, or Swiss alpine shrieking,
That grates on your nerves from Geneva to Peking.

Z is for Zurich, and why not append,
That Zurich's a city, and really

THE END

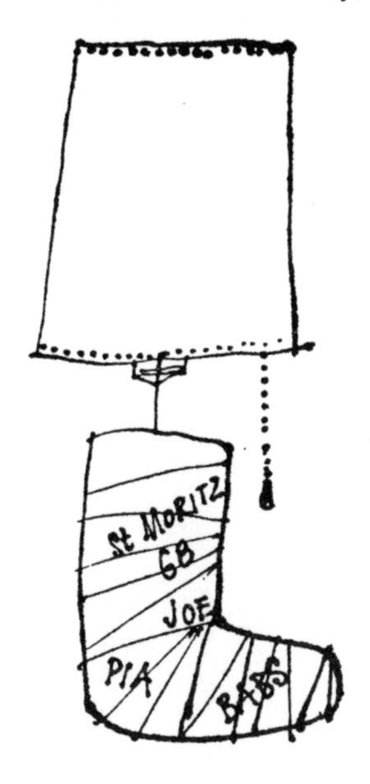

The author wishes to express his sincere appreciation to the editors of the magazine *Switzerland* (Swiss National Tourist Office) and the Swissair *Gazette*, in whose pages many of these pieces first appeared.